THE SPANISH BORDERLANDS

TEXTBOOK EDITION

∵

THE YALE CHRONICLES
OF AMERICA SERIES
ALLEN JOHNSON
EDITOR

GERHARD R. LOMER
CHARLES W. JEFFERYS
ASSISTANT EDITORS

THE
SPANISH BORDERLANDS

A CHRONICLE OF OLD
FLORIDA AND THE SOUTHWEST
BY HERBERT E. BOLTON

TORONTO: GLASGOW, BROOK & CO.
NEW YORK: UNITED STATES PUBLISHERS
ASSOCIATION, INC.

Printed in the United States of America

PREFACE

THIS book is to tell of Spanish pathfinders and pioneers in the regions between Florida and California, now belonging to the United States, over which Spain held sway for centuries. These were the northern outposts of New Spain, maintained chiefly to hold the country against foreign intruders and against the inroads of savage tribes. They were far from the centers of Spanish colonial civilization, in the West Indies, Central America, Mexico, and Peru.

The rule of Spain has passed; but her colonies have grown into independent nations. From Mexico to Chile, throughout half of America, the Spanish language and Spanish institutions are still dominant. Even in the old borderlands north of the Río Grande, the imprint of Spain's sway is still deep and clear. The names of four States — Florida, Colorado, Nevada, and California — are

Spanish in form. Scores of rivers and mountains and hundreds of towns and cities in the United States still bear the names of saints dear to the Spanish pioneers. Southwestern Indians yet speak Spanish in preference to English. Scores of the towns have Spanish quarters, where the life of the old days still goes on and where the soft Castilian tongue is still spoken. Southwestern English has been enriched by Spanish contact, and hundreds of words of Spanish origin are in current use in speech and print everywhere along the border.

Throughout these Hispanic regions now in Anglo-American hands, Spanish architecture is still conspicuous. Scattered all the way from Georgia to San Francisco are the ruins of Spanish missions. Others dating from the old régime are yet well preserved and are in daily use as chapels. From belfries in Florida, Texas, New Mexico, Arizona, and California, still sound bells cast in Spain and bearing the royal arms. In many of the towns, and here and there in open country, old-time adobes are still to be seen. Moreover, the Spanish element has furnished the *motif* for a new type of architecture in the Southwest that has become one of the most distinctive American possessions. In California, Texas, and Arizona, the type is dominated by mission architecture. In New Mexico it is strongly modified by the native culture which found expression in pueblo building.

There are still other marks of Spanish days on the southern border. We see them in social, religious, economic, and even in legal customs. California has her Portolá festival, her *rodeos*, and her Mission Play. Everywhere in the Southwest there are quaint church customs brought from Spain or Mexico by the early pioneers. From the Spaniard the American cowboy inherited his trade, his horse, his outfit, his vocabulary, and his methods. Spain is stamped on the land surveys. From Sacramento to St. Augustine nearly everybody holds his land by a title going back to Mexico or Madrid. Most of the farms along the border are divisions of famous grants which are still known by their original Spanish names. In the realm of law, principles regarding mines, water rights on streams, and the property rights of women — to mention only a few — have been retained from the Spanish régime in the Southwest. Not least has been the Hispanic appeal to the imagination. The Spanish occupation has stamped the literature of the borderlands and has furnished theme and color for a myriad of writers, great and small. Nor is this Hispanic cult — or culture — losing its hold. On the contrary, it is growing stronger. In short, the Southwest is as Spanish in color and historical background as New England is Puritan, as New York is Dutch, or as New Orleans is French.

My original manuscript for this book was written on a much larger scale than the Editor desired. In the work of reduction and rewriting, to fit it for the Series, I have had the able assistance of Miss Constance Lindsay Skinner.

H. E. B.

UNIVERSITY OF CALIFORNIA,
October, 1920.

CONTENTS

The Explorers

The Colonies

CONTENTS

THE SPANISH BORDERLANDS

∴

CHAPTER I

PONCE DE LEÓN, AYLLÓN, AND NARVÁEZ

THE sixteenth century dawned auspiciously for Spain. After eight hundred years of warfare with the infidel usurpers of the Peninsula, the last Moslem stronghold had fallen; and, through the union of Aragon and Castile, all Spain was united under one crown and lifted to the peak of power in Europe. To the world about her, Spain presented the very image of unity, wealth, and power, adamantine and supreme.

But the image of serene absolutism is always a portent of calamity. There followed a period of brilliant achievement abroad, while the prosperity of the nation at home steadily declined. Taxation was exorbitant. Industry declined because of the lack of skilled workers, for the expulsion of the

Moors had robbed Spain of artisans and pastoral laborers. The nobles and gentry were swordsmen, crusaders, and spoilers of the Egyptians — made such by centuries of war with the Moors — and they held all labor and trade in scorn.

Each year, more of the gold which annually poured into the Emperor's lap must needs be poured out again for products which were no longer grown or manufactured within the realm. Gold was the monarch's need; gold was the dazzling lure which the warrior nobles of Spain followed. There were no longer Egyptians at home to spoil. To the New World must these warrior nobles now look for work for their swords and for wealth without menial toil or the indignities of commerce. Only on that far frontier could they hope to enjoy the personal liberty and something of their old feudal powers, now curtailed by absolutism at home. Irked by restrictions and surveillance as well as by inaction or poverty, these sons of the sword sought again on this soil the freedom which was once the Spaniard's birthright.

Adventure, conquest, piety, wealth, were the ideals of those Spanish explorers, who, pushing northward from the West Indies and from the City of Mexico, first planted the Cross and the banner of Spain in the swamps of Florida and in the arid plateaus of New Mexico. The conquistadors who threaded the unknown way through the American wilderness were armored knights upon armored horses; proud, stern, hardy, and courageous; men of punctilious honor, loyal to King and Mother Church, humble only before the symbols of their Faith; superstitious — believing in portents and omens no less than in the mysteries of the Church, for the magic of Moorish soothsayers and astrologers had colored the life of their ancestors for generations.

Part pagan, however, the conquistador was no less a zealous warrior for Church and King. His face was as flint against all heretics. He went forth for the heathen's gold and the heathen's soul. If he succeeded, riches and honor were his. Hardship, peril, death, had no terrors for this soldier-knight. If he was pitiless towards others, so was he pitiless toward himself. He saw his mission enveloped with romantic glory. Such men were the conquistadors, who, after the capture of the Aztec capital in the summer of 1521, carried the Spanish banner northward.

While Cortés was still wrestling with the Aztecs, Spanish expeditions were moving out from the West Indies — Española (Hayti), Cuba, Porto

Rico, and Jamaica. These islands are well called the nursery of Spanish culture in the Western Hemisphere. By 1513 there were seventeen towns on Española alone, in which the life of Old Spain was reproduced in form, though reflecting the colors of savage environment. Mines were worked by enslaved natives; grain was sown and harvested; cotton and sugar-cane were cultivated. The slave trade in negroes and Indians flourished. Friars cared for the souls of the faithful. The harbor winds were winged with Spanish sails, homeward bound with rich cargoes, or set towards the coast of the mysterious continent which should one day disclose to the persistent mariner an open strait leading westward to Cathay. In the midst of the crudities of a frontier, hidalgo and official of Española lived joyously and with touches of Oriental magnificence. Gold! It lay in glittering heaps upon their dicing-tables. It stung not only their imaginations but their palates — so we learn from the description of a banquet given by one of them, at which, to the music of players brought from Spain, the guests salted their savory meats with gold dust. Is it to be marveled at that men of such hardy digestions should have conquered a wilderness bravely and gayly?

Among these romantic exiles at Española was Juan Ponce de León — John of the Lion's Paunch — who had come to the island with Columbus in 1493, as a member of the first permanent colony. In Ponce's veins flowed the bluest blood of Spain. His family could be traced back to the twelfth century.

Rumors of gold drew Ponce to Porto Rico (1508), which island he "pacified," after the very thorough Spanish manner, sharing the honors of valor with the famous dog, Bercerillo. This dog, according to the old historian, Herrera, "made wonderful havock among these people, and knew which of them were in war and which in peace, like a man; for which reason the Indians were more afraid of ten Spaniards with the dog, than of one hundred without him, and therefore he had one share and a half of all that was taken allowed him, as was done to one that carried a crossbow, as well in gold as slaves and other things, which his master received. Very extraordinary things were reported of this dog."[1]

Ponce was made Governor of Porto Rico, but was almost immediately removed, as the appointment had been made over the head of Don Diego Columbus, Governor of Española. Thus dispossessed of office, Ponce sought fame, and wealth, and

[1] Lowery, *Spanish Settlements*, p. 133.

perpetual youth, perhaps, in exploration. "It is true," writes Herrera, the royal chronicler, "that besides the principal aim of Juan Ponce de León in the expedition which he undertook, which was to discover new lands, . . . another was to seek the fountain of Bimini and a certain river of Florida. It was said and believed by the Indians of Cuba and Española that by bathing in the river or the fountain, old men became youths." What more was needed to fire the blood of an adventurer like Ponce, who already possessed influence and a fortune? Nothing, as the event proved. By means of his friends he obtained a patent from King Charles (1512), later Emperor Charles V, authorizing him to seek and govern the island of Bimini, which rumor placed to the northwest.

What Ponce hoped to accomplish in the enterprise, and also the aims of his brother conquerors, can be gathered from his patent. If Ponce was an explorer and adventurer, he, like the others, hoped also to be a colonizer, a transplanter of Spanish people and of Spanish civilization. Whoever fails to understand this, fails to understand the patriotic aim of the Spanish pioneers in America. The Catholic monarchs were a thrifty pair, and they made the business of conquest pay for itself. The successes of men like Columbus and Cortés played into their hands. Every expedition was regarded as a good gamble. The expenses of exploration therefore were charged to the adventurer, under promise of great rewards, in titles and profits from the enterprise, if any there might be. Under these circumstances the sovereigns lost little in any case, and they might win untold returns. And so with Ponce. By the terms of his grant he was empowered to equip a fleet, at his own expense, people Bimini with Spaniards, exploit its wealth, and, as *adelantado*, govern it in the name of the sovereign. In keeping with the method already in vogue in the West Indies, the natives were to be distributed among the discoverers and settlers, that they might be protected, christianized, civilized, and, sad to say, exploited. Though the intent of this last provision in the royal patents of the day was benevolent, the practical result to the natives was usually disastrous.

With a fleet of three vessels, on March 3, 1513, Ponce sailed from Porto Rico and anchored a month later on the coast of the northern mainland, near the mouth of the St. John's River. Here he landed, took formal possession of the "island," and named it La Florida, because of its verdant beauty

and because it was discovered in the Easter season.
After sailing northward for a day, Ponce turned
south again.   Twice in landing on the coast he and
his men were set upon by the natives.   On Sunday,
the 8th of May, he doubled Cape Cañaveral, called
by him the Cape of the Currents; and by the fif-
teenth he was coasting along the Florida Keys.
The strain of romance in these old explorers is well
illustrated by the name which Ponce, seeker of the
Fountain of Youth, gave to the Florida Keys.
"The Martyrs," he called them, because the high
rocks, at a distance, looked "like men who are
suffering."

Ponce sailed up the western shore of the peninsula, perhaps as far north as Pensacola Bay, before he again turned southward, still unaware that
Florida was not an island.   Anchored off the southern end of Florida, he allowed himself to fall into a
snare set for him by natives.   These natives told
an interesting story.   There was nearby, they said,
a cacique named Carlos whose land fairly sprouted
gold.   While Ponce and his officers were drinking
in the splendid tale, the Indians were massing
canoes for an attack on the Spanish ships.   Two
battles followed before the painted warriors were
driven off and the Spaniards sailed homeward

without either a sight of gold or a taste of the
magic spring. But his voyage was not fruitless,
for on the way back to Española Ponce made a valuable find. He discovered the Bahama Channel,
which later became the route for treasure ships returning to Spain from the West Indies. It was to
protect this channel that Florida eventually had to
be colonized.

Ponce proceeded at once to Spain, where he
"went about like a person of importance, because
his qualities merited it." From the King he received another patent (1514) authorizing him to
colonize not only "Bimini," which one of his ships
was said to have discovered, but the "Island of
Florida" as well. Just now, however, renewed complaints came in of terrible devastations wrought
upon Spanish colonies by the Caribs of the Lesser
Antilles. Ponce was put in command of a fleet
to subdue these ferocious savages, and his plans
for Florida were delayed seven years.

Meanwhile other expeditions from the West Indies found Florida to be part of the mainland. By
1519, indeed, the entire coast of the Gulf between
Yucatán and Florida had been explored and
charted, thus ending the Spanish hope of finding
there a strait leading westward to India. Chief

among these explorers of the Gulf was the good
pilot Pineda, agent of the governor of Jamaica. He
mapped the coast of Amichel — as the Spaniards
called the Texas coast — and was the one to discover the mouth of that large river flowing into the
Gulf which he named the Espíritu Santo, but which
we know today as the Mississippi. This was
twenty-two years before De Soto crossed the Father of Waters near Memphis. Amichel was a
wondrous land, indeed, according to the reports
dispatched to Spain by Pineda's master. It had
gold in plenty and two distinct native races, giants
and pygmies.

At last Ponce returned to his task. On February 10, 1521, at Porto Rico, he wrote to King
Charles: "Among my services I discovered at my
own cost and charge, the Island of Florida and
others in its district . . . and now I return to
that Island, if it please God's will, to settle it."[1]
According to Herrera, the rare old chronicler, it was
emulation of the conqueror of Mexico that aroused
Ponce to make this venture. For now "the name
of Hernando Cortés was on everybody's lips and

---

[1] Lowery, *Spanish Settlements*, p. 158, quoting Shea's translation in Winsor, *Narrative and Critical History of America*, vol. II.
p. 234.

his fame was great." In February, then, Ponce again set sail, with two ships, two hundred men, fifty horses, a number of other domestic animals, and farm implements to cultivate the soil. By the King's command, monks and priests accompanied him for missionary work among the natives.

Ponce landed on the Florida coast, probably in the neighborhood of Charlotte Harbor, where, on his earlier voyage, the natives had regaled him with fables of the golden realm of Carlos, the cacique, and had attacked his ships. Since then slave-hunting raids along their coast had filled these warlike, freedom-loving Florida natives with an intense hatred for Spanish invaders. Hardly had the colonists begun to build houses when the Indians set upon them with fury. The valiant Ponce, leading his men in a counter attack, received an Indian arrow in his body. Some of his followers were killed. This disaster put an end to the enterprise. Ponce and his colonists departed and made port at Cuba, having lost a ship on the way. A few days later Ponce died from his wounds, leaving unsolved the mystery of the Fountain of Youth. Over his grave in Porto Rico, where his body was sent for burial, his epitaph was thus inscribed:

> Here rest the bones of a LION,
> Mightier in deeds than in name.[1]

So perished the discoverer and first foreign ruler of Florida, as many another standard-bearer of the white race on this soil was to perish, from the dart of the irreconcilable Indian. The conquest of the Aztecs, living in permanent towns, proved comparatively easy for Cortés, with his superior means of waging war; but the subjection of the northern tribes, who had no fixed abodes, who wandered over hundreds of miles in hunting and war, was another task. Europeans began the conquest of America by seizing the Indians and selling them into slavery. It is an oft-repeated boast that tyranny has never thrived on American soil, but it is seldom remembered that the first battles for freedom in this land were fought by the red natives.

Meanwhile a new star arose to beckon explorers northward. A new region had been discovered far up the eastern coast by adventurers who were spying about Florida while Ponce was absent at the Carib wars. Chief of these interlopers was Lucas

[1] "Mole sub hac fortis Requiescunt ossa LEONIS
Qui Vicit factis Nomina magna suis."
Lowery, *Spanish Settlements*, p. **160**.

Vásquez de Ayllón, an *oidor*, or superior judge, of Española, who took into his service one Francisco Gordillo and sent him out to explore. Gordillo met in the Bahamas a slave hunter named Quexos, and the two joined company. Thus it happened that in June, 1521, about the time that Ponce was driven from Florida, these two adventurers landed in a region, called Chicora by the natives, which seems to have been near the Cape Fear River on the Carolina coast. After taking formal possession of the country, they coaxed one hundred and fifty of their red-skinned hosts on board and sailed away to sell them in Santo Domingo. This time a rude shock awaited the slave hunters. When they reached the capital they were ordered by Governor Diego Columbus to set the Indians free and return them to their native land. Don Diego deserves remembrance as a liberator.

Among the captives, however, there was one whom the Spaniards detained. They baptized him Francisco Chicorana, and Ayllón took him as his personal servant. Francisco was a choice wag. Doubtless because he desired to be taken home, he employed his time and talents in regaling his captors with romances of Chicora. He was taken by Ayllón to Spain, where two famous historians,

Peter Martyr and Oviedo, got from him at first hand and preserved for us these earliest tales of Carolina.

According to Francisco the natives of Chicora were white, with brown hair hanging to their heels. In the country there were pearls and other precious stones. There were domesticated deer, which lived in the houses of the natives and generously furnished them milk and cheese. The people were governed by a giant king called Datha, whose enormous size was not natural but had been produced by softening and stretching his bones in childhood. He told, too, of a race of men with inflexible tails, "like the tailed Englishmen of Kent," says a Spanish humorist. "This tail was not movable like those of quadrupeds, but formed one mass, as is the case with fish and crocodiles, and was as hard as bone. When these men wished to sit down, they had consequently to have a seat with an open bottom; and if there were none, they had to dig a hole more than a cubit deep to hold their tails and allow them to rest." If any one be disposed to doubt these stories let him ponder well what Peter Martyr says: "Each may accept or reject my account as he chooses. Envy is a plague natural to the human race, always seeking to depreciate and to search for weeds in another's garden. . . . This pest afflicts the foolish, or persons devoid of literary culture, who live useless lives like cumberers of the earth."[1]

Encouraged by these yarns, in 1523 Ayllón obtained from Charles V the desired patent to Chicora, the land of the Giant King. As in the case of Bimini, the project was a gamble, and, like Ponce, Ayllón put up the money. Chicora was not the sole objective. Ayllón was to continue his explorations north for eight hundred leagues, or until he found the strait leading westward to Asia, which, if found, must be explored. Of the lands discovered he was to be *adelantado*, or governor. He was to have for himself in full ownership an estate fifteen leagues square — a round million acres. He was to take with him, at the royal expense, friars to convert the Indians, and, in view of the sad results in the islands, Indians were not to be parceled out or forced to work. Experience was having its effect on the royal policy.

Three years passed before Ayllón was ready to take possession of his domain, but in the interval further explorations along the coast were made by his pilot Quexos, who brought back glowing

[1] *De Orbe Novo* (ed. by F. A. MacNutt) vol. ii, pp. 258-59.

reports of gold, silver, and pearls. And at the same time Esteban Gómez, a pilot who had been with Magellan — and had deserted him — came out from Spain, looking for the northern strait, and sailed the American coast between Nova Scotia and Florida. Thus, by the year 1525, Spanish navigators had explored the entire shore line from Cape Breton to Cape Horn.

At length, in July, 1526, Ayllón sailed from Española with six vessels carrying five hundred men and women from the islands, some black slaves, eighty-nine horses, and other equipment for the colony. It was a force larger than that with which Cortés had invaded Mexico. There were also three Dominican friars; for, wrote the King, "Our principal intent in the discovery of new lands is that the inhabitants and natives thereof, who are without the light or knowledge of the faith, may be brought to understand the truths of our Holy Catholic Faith, that they may come to a knowledge thereof and become Christians and be saved, and this is the chief motive that you are to bear and hold in this affair."[1]

[1] Lowery, *Spanish Settlements*, p. 162. From Shea's translation in *The Catholic Church in Colonial Days*, p. 105.

Ayllón anchored his ships at the mouth of a river, probably the Cape Fear, which, with romantic optimism, he named the Jordan. In making port he lost one of his ships with its cargo, and this led to the construction on the spot of an open boat with one mast, to be propelled by both oars and sail. Here we have the first shipbuilding of record in the United States. From this place exploring parties went out by sea and others pushed a short way inland. A misfortune now befell Ayllón. His interpreter, the romancer, Francisco Chicorana, seized the opportunity so long waited for and deserted to his people. Ayllón was thus unable to talk to the Chicorans and convince them of his friendly intent. This region, however, about a dangerous harbor, looked uninviting, and no more was needed than the news of a pleasanter land, brought by returning explorers, to start Ayllón and his colonists southward. Down the coast they all went to the mouth of the Pedee River — the Gualdape, Ayllón called it — and there began the settlement of San Miguel de Gualdape.

But the settlement came quickly to grief. The blasts of an exceptionally cold winter struck down many of the colonists. Provisions gave out. The settlers were too weakened by exposure and disease to catch the fish which abounded in the river. Ayllón himself sank under the hardship and privation; and, on St. Luke's Day, October 18, 1526, he died. Quarrels ensued among the survivors. Mutineers under an ambitious officer imprisoned the lieutenant who succeeded Ayllón in command; and, in turn, negro slaves rose and fired the house of the usurper. Indians, encouraged by the domestic imbroglio, made attacks and killed some of the Spaniards. It was now resolved to abandon the colony and return to Santo Domingo. About a hundred and fifty enfeebled and destitute men and women set sail in midwinter, towing after them the body of their dead commander in the one-masted craft they had built. As they made their slow way homeward, seven men were frozen to death on board one of the ships. The icy winds and sea, which lashed the small vessels about and took the lives of these emaciated sailors, took also their toll of the dead. The boat bearing Ayllón's body was swept away; and, weighted full with water, it sank, says Oviedo the historian, in "the sepulchre of the ocean-sea where have been and shall be put other captains and governors."

Florida and Chicora: these were still but names, but names now heightened in romance by the tragic deaths of Ponce and Ayllón and by new tales heard in the wilderness.

The Northern Mystery was still unsolved, and it was not long before another attempt was made to settle Florida. The enterprise was undertaken this time by Pánfilo de Narváez, the same Narváez who in 1520 had been sent to Vera Cruz to arrest disobedient Cortés, and had lost an eye and suffered captivity for his pains.[1] Narváez was a native of Valladolid, of good blood and gentle breeding. He had taken part in the conquest of Cuba. He is described as a tall man of proud mien, with a fair complexion, a red beard, and — since the encounter with Cortés — one eagle eye. His manner was diplomatic and gracious and his voice resonant, "as if it came from a cave."[2] He had acquired wealth in the New World (and a reputation for keeping his money) as well as sound fame as a soldier, for he was said to be "brave *against Indians* and probably would have been against any people, had ever occasion offered for fighting them."[2]

In June, 1527, Narváez sailed from Spain with six hundred colonists and a number of Franciscan

[1] See *The Spanish Conquerors*, in this Series.

[2] Lowery, *Spanish Settlements*, p. 174. Both quotations from Bernal Díaz, repeated by Lowery.

friars.   Among his officers was Alvar Nuñez Cabeza de Vaca, of whom more anon.   Narváez's patent gave him the country from the Río de las Palmas to the Cape of Florida, and thus made him heir to part of the land — as well as to the misfortunes — of Ponce de León.   His misfortunes began in the West Indies.   At Santo Domingo a fourth of his colonists deserted; and two ships which he had sent to Trinidad, with Cabeza de Vaca, were wrecked in a hurricane.   The fears thus spread amongst his company forced him to remain at anchor until the passing of winter.   The spring of 1528 saw his expedition, its personnel now reduced to about four hundred, on the way.   Strong winds from the south drove his ships to the Florida coast and on Good Friday he landed at Tampa Bay. There he found a village, from which the natives had fled at sight of his sails.   And in one of the deserted houses he saw a faint glint of the hope which kindled the heart of every explorer — a small golden ornament dropped in the flight.

Before this tenantless village Narváez unfurled the royal standard and recited a proclamation prepared by learned jurists of Spain wherewith to acquaint the Indians of the King's lands with their new estate.   But the natives ignored its benign provisions and plain warnings. They returned next day and "made signs and menaces, and appeared to say we must go away from the country." Narváez, however, having come as the servant of the Crown and to fill his own coffers, was in no mind to retreat. Somewhere in that wilderness there must be gold. What was that yellow-gleaming ornament he had found? Indeed, there was a land to the north, named Appalachen, teeming with gold; so the natives said. He decided to send the fleet up the coast, to find a good harbor and there await him. He and his officers with their wives, the friars, and the colonists, would press inland to seek Appalachen. In this decision Narváez ignored the advice of Vaca, who said that they and their ships would never meet again, and the warnings of one of the women. This woman had foretold in Spain many of the circumstances of the voyage and now declared that horrible disaster would befall the inland explorers; for so had a Moorish soothsayer in Castile prognosticated. This sibyl and the other wives insisted on going with the ships. The voyage having begun, they immediately took to themselves new husbands, knowing, by the Moor's prophecy, that never more should they salute their lawful spouses.

Narváez's company, now reft of its women, comprised three hundred men, including five priests and forty officers and soldiers in armor, mounted upon armored horses. Led by the standard-bearer, this shining host plunged into the Florida wilds. Crossing the Withlacoochee and Suwanee Rivers, they passed from a fairly open country into dense forests. Their food gave out and they nourished themselves and their horses as best they could on the shoots of young palm. Men and horses were exhausted from hunger and fatigue and galled from the heavy armor, when at last on St. John's Day (June 24, 1528), they reached Appalachen, near the present Tallahassee in northern Florida. But golden Appalachen proved to be only a town of forty clay huts, occupied then by women and children; for the men were away on the warpath. The Spaniards took possession of the town and fed on maize for twenty-five days, obliged occasionally to do battle against the returning warriors. Excursions into the surrounding country, attended by skirmishes, convinced Narváez that there was no great and rich city there which might answer to the false description given him of Appalachen. "Thenceforth were great lakes, dense mountains, immense deserts and solitudes." So Narváez and his company turned south again and westward in the hope of finding their ships. After nine days' difficult march they came upon Auté, another deserted Indian village, where again they found food. They reached the sea at last at Appalachee Bay.

But there was no sign of the ships. The ships, in fact, had sailed away to Cuba. Yet the sea was their only hope; so they determined to slay their horses for food and to build a fleet of horsehide boats in which to escape to Pánuco (Mexico) which was thought to be close by. Little did they dream that it was over a thousand miles away.

There was only one carpenter in the company. They had, says Vaca, "no tools, nor iron, nor forge, nor tow, nor resin, nor rigging." But necessity is the mother of invention, and Robinson Crusoe could scarcely have done better himself. Bellows were contrived from wooden tubes and deerskin. Nails, saws, and axes were made of the iron from the stirrups, crossbows, and spurs. Palmettos were used in place of tow. From the pitch of the pines a Greek made resin for calking, and the boats were covered with horsehide. Ropes and rigging were made from palmetto fiber and horsehair, sails from the shirts of the men, and oars from young savins. While the boats were building four journeys were made to Auté for maize, and every third day a horse was killed for food. The skins of the horses' legs were removed entire, tanned, and used for water bottles. In the course of this work ten men were slain by Indians, and forty others died from disease and hunger. At last five boats were completed, each twenty-one cubits long. By the 22d of September the last horse was eaten, and on that day two hundred and forty-two men set sail in those five frail craft of horsehide, not one among them knowing how to handle a boat. In memory of the diet of horseflesh they named the harbor where they embarked the Bay of Horses.

Rowing along the coast, occasionally passing a village of fishermen — "a poor miserable lot," says Vaca — at the end of thirty days they were detained at an island by a storm. Next day they had a battle with some Indians near a large inlet, perhaps Pensacola Bay. Three or four days farther west a Greek and a negro went ashore for food and fresh water and never returned. [1]   Farther along the coast they came to the mouth of a large river, no doubt the Mississippi. The combined strength of its current and of a storm which now arose was

[1] Eleven years later De Soto found the Greek's dagger in the possession of Indians near Mobile Bay

so great that the flotilla was driven far out to sea, and the boats became separated and were never again all together. It is known, however, from Vaca's narrative that they again drew in to the shore. Three of them, Vaca's boat and two others, were wrecked, on the 6th of November, on an island — Galveston Island, or one near it, by Vaca named Malhado, or Misfortune. Another boat, carrying the commissary and the friars, was wrecked on the mainland farther west.

One of the five boats yet remained afloat, the commander's own. Narváez bore on westward, hugging the coast. One day he descried on land some of the castaways of the fourth boat which had been wrecked, making their way painfully on foot. He landed some of his own crew to lighten his boat and proceeded by water, while the destitute band with the friars marched slowly along the shore. At evening he hove to, after ferrying the pedestrians across a bay that cut off their route, and landed the rest of his people. Dropping a stone for anchor, Narváez then prepared to spend the night in his boat with his page, who was dangerously ill. But a wild wind came down with the dark and swept his frail craft out upon the deep. And Narváez followed Ayllón to "sepulchre in the ocean-sea."

CHAPTER II

CABEZA DE VACA

ALVAR NUÑEZ CABEZA DE VACA, now a castaway on "Malhado" Island, on the wild coast of Texas, was a noble of old lineage. He had relinquished high official position in Spain to join Narváez in his adventure. Of the disaster and its remarkable sequel Vaca wrote a circumstantial account which enables us to get his story at first hand. On the island Vaca took command of his comrades in adversity. His first need was to learn if the country was inhabited. So he ordered Lope de Oviedo, who had "more strength and was stouter than any of the rest," to climb a tree to spy out the land. Oviedo discovered Indians and brought them to where the Spaniards lay shivering and exhausted on the beach, some of them too frail to crawl among the rocks for shelter from the biting winds. The castaways must have looked forlorn, indeed; for Vaca, who had a nice literary touch, says that their bodies had "become the perfect figures of death"; and that the Indians "at sight of what had befallen us, and our state of suffering and melancholy destitution . . . began to lament so earnestly that they might have been heard at a distance and continued so doing more than half an hour." Even in his weakness and misery, for Vaca was in a worse condition than many of his companions, his imagination was caught by the strange scene those savages "wild and untaught" presented as they sat among the white men "howling like brutes over our misfortunes." Vaca besought the Indians to take the Spaniards to their dwellings. Thirty savages loaded themselves with driftwood and immediately set off at a run for their camp some distance away. The other Indians, holding up the emaciated white men so that their feet barely touched the ground, followed in short swift marches, pausing occasionally to warm the Spaniards at great fires built by the thirty wood carriers at intervals along the trail. In the village they lodged their guests in huts where they had also built fires, fed them with roasted fish and roots, and sang and danced and wept about them until far into the night. In the morning they brought more cooked fish and in all ways showed much hospitality.

The very next day, much to his delight, Vaca learned that other white men were on the same island. A messenger being sent out, soon Vaca was joined at the village by some of his former companions, Dorantes, Castillo, and their men, who had been wrecked on the island the day before Vaca landed there. Three of the castaways, numbering at this time about eighty, had been drowned in an ineffectual attempt to recover one of the horsehide boats. Terrible as the sea had been to them, they would have dared its storms once more in the desperate hope of coming at last somewhere into a Spanish harbor.

As December waned, bitter cold and heavy storms descended on this coast, stopped the fish supply, and prevented the Indians from digging for the edible roots which grew under water. Starvation and exposure thinned the ranks of the Spaniards. The survivors, to the horror of the Indians, ate the flesh of their own dead. When spring came, Vaca had with him but fifteen men.

A new danger now assailed them. Disease attacked the Indians and destroyed half their number. In their panic the natives accused the Spaniards of having brought the plague upon them by occult means; and they were only prevented from slaying them by the chief who had taken Vaca in charge. If, argued this worthy, the white men could bring the disease upon the Indians, they could also surely have prevented their own people from dying. And "God our Lord willed that the others should heed this opinion and counsel, and be hindered in their design." So the Indians did not kill the Spaniards. But the notion that their mysterious refugees possessed supernatural powers was too pleasant to be given up. Now let those powers be used to cure sick Indians and banish the plague. As Vaca puts it, with his occasional sly touch of humor, "they wished to make us physicians, without examination or inquiring for diplomas." In vain he tried to laugh the savages out of their conviction. They replied that when stones and "other matters growing about the fields have virtue" then certainly "extraordinary men" must be more highly endowed. And if those extraordinary men would not heal, neither should they eat. This was cogent reasoning. After hungering for several days Vaca took the first step towards the remarkable career he was to follow later on as a Medicine Man. He had observed the Indian witch-doctors blowing upon their patients and passing their hands over them, frequently with successful results. And, devoutly religious as he was, he knew that in his homeland the "prayer of faith" uttered by humble petitioners before the wayside shrines frequently wrought the recovery of the sick. Therefore, he seems to have reasoned, a blend of Indian and Christian faiths should be efficacious here. He says:

Our method was to bless the sick, breathing upon them and recite a Pater-noster and an Ave Maria, praying with all earnestness to God our Lord that he would give health and influence them to make us some good return. In His clemency He willed that all those for whom we supplicated should tell the others that they were sound and in health, directly after we made the sign of the blessed cross over them. For this the Indians treated us kindly; they deprived themselves of food that they might give to us, and presented us with skins and some trifles.

Scarcity of food continued so that sometimes Indians and white men went without eating for several days at a time. Presently an Indian guide, who had been bribed by a marten skin, departed westward along the mainland coast, taking with him all the Spaniards but three, Vaca, Oviedo, and Alaniz, who were too frail for travel. In the summer Vaca went with the Indians to the mainland foraging for food. The life he led was "insupportable," being practically that of a slave. One of his

duties was to dig out the edible roots from below
the water and from among the cane. His fingers
were so worn from this labor that "did a straw
but touch them they would bleed"; and the sharp
spikes of broken cane tore his naked flesh.

For nearly six years Vaca lived a slave among
these Indians. He had long intended to escape and
to set off westward "in quest of Christians"; for,
somewhere towards the sunset, lay Pánuco, and,
given bodily strength, a brave heart, and faith in
God, a man might hope to reach it. But Vaca
would not leave his two companions. Then Alaniz
died; and Oviedo, however much "stouter" than
the other Spaniards in the matter of climbing trees,
was not of stout courage. He feared to be left
behind and he would not go. Every winter Vaca
returned to the island and entreated him to pluck
up heart; and every spring Oviedo put him off, but
promised that next year he would set out.

Vaca did not let time pass unimproved. To get
rid of root-digging and sore fingers, he decided to
enter the domain of commerce. He could begin
with good prospects because the Indians of the
mainland had already heard flattering reports of
his skill as a Medicine Man. And perhaps he expected to fit himself for the journey down the coast

by acquiring a number of Indian dialects, by becoming a connoisseur of Indian staples and trinkets, and by learning from western tribes on their
summer buffalo hunts in Texas some details of the
country through which he must pass on his projected journey to Pánuco. Ordinary perils and
hardships had lost their terrors for Vaca. Roving
naked and barefooted like the tribesmen, his body
had become inured to fatigues and to wind and
weather; periods of famine had also prepared this
erstwhile son of magnificence and luxury to cope
with the barren wilderness when the day of escape
he had waited for should come at last. He had
learned to make the Indians' weapons and to use
them in hunting, though, as he admits, he never
developed the Indian's subtlety in trailing. He
was so satisfactory as a servant, indeed, that his
masters were content to have him do their trading
for them; and they let him come and go at will. Of
his career as a merchant in Texas, Vaca gives a
lengthy account, interesting because it is the first
record of trade in this now great commercial land.

I set to trafficking, and strove to make my employ-
ment profitable in the ways I could best contrive, and
by that means I got food and good treatment. The Indians would beg me to go from one quarter to another

for things of which they have need; for in consequence of incessant hostilities, they cannot traverse
the country, nor make many exchanges. With my
merchandise and trade I went into the interior as far
as I pleased, and travelled along the coast forty or fifty
leagues. The principal wares were cones and other
pieces of sea-snail, conchs used for cutting, and fruit
like a bean of the highest value among them, which
they use as a medicine and employ in their dances and
festivities. . . . Such were what I carried into the
interior; and in barter I got and brought back skins,
ochre with which they rub and color the face, hard
canes of which to make arrows, sinews, cement and
flint for the heads, and tassels of the hair of deer that
by dyeing they make red. This occupation suited me
well; for the travel allowed me liberty to go where I
wished, I was not obliged to work, and was not a slave.

Evidently he made an enviable name for himself
among the savages as a merchant of their primitive
commerce for, wherever he went, he received fair
treatment and generous hospitality "out of regard
to my commodities"; and those Indians with whom
he had not traded, hearing of him, "sought and
desired the acquaintance for my reputation." He
traveled far afield in pursuit of his "leading object
while journeying in this business," which was to
find the best way to go forward. "The hardships
that I underwent in this were long to tell, as well of
peril and privation as of storms and cold," he

writes: "Oftentimes they overtook me alone and in the wilderness; but I came forth from them all by the great mercy of God our Lord."

Three times Vaca saw "cattle" and tasted their meat. And he has contributed to historical narrative the first description of the American buffalo:

I think they are about the size of those in Spain. They have small horns like the cows of Morocco; the hair is very long and flocky like the merinos. Some are tawny, others black. To my judgment the flesh is finer and fatter than that of this country [Spain]. Of the skins of those not full grown the Indians make blankets, and of the larger they make shoes [moccasins] and bucklers. They come as far as the seacoast of Florida, from a northerly direction, ranging through a tract of more than four hundred leagues; and throughout the whole region over which they run, the people who inhabit near, descend and live upon them, distributing a vast many hides into the interior country.

From these travels Vaca returned each year to the island to see how Oviedo fared and to urge him again to dare the wilderness with him. History gives us few instances of greater loyalty than Vaca's. It was not in him to deal with comrades as Narváez had dealt with his followers after leaving the Bay of Horses, saying that "each should do what he thought best to save his own life; that he so intended to act." At last Vaca overcame Oviedo's timidity and the two men set forth. Perhaps Vaca swam to the mainland with Oviedo on his back, or towed him over on a piece of driftwood; for he says, "I got him off, crossing him over the bay, and over four rivers in the coast, as he could not swim." The two men were naked, armed only with bows and arrows and conch-shell knives, and Vaca carried his trader's pack of shell trinkets. After crossing the fourth river they went to the sea at Matagorda Bay, where they met with a tribe whom Vaca calls the Quevenes. These Indians told him that they had seen men like himself in the custody of another tribe farther down the coast. Vaca knew that the men must be his old companions, who had left the island four years previously; and he resolved at once to seek them and with them to escape. But this new peril in prospect, added to the rough manner of the Quevenes, was too much for the timid soul of Oviedo. And, deaf to all Vaca's imploring, he turned back toward the island — and out of history — leaving the man who had stood by him so faithfully to pursue his dangerous way alone. Who knows but that some giant Karankawa chief, of those who in the nineteenth century pestered Austin's colonists in Texas, was a descendant of this Oviedo?

The Quevenes intended to hold Vaca as a slave; but he slipped away and stole out along the river bank — the Colorado, it seems — where, as he had heard, the Indians who had white men with them were gathering pecans for their winter's food store. Here he found Dorantes and Castillo and a Christianized Moor named Estevanico. These three were all that now remained of the twelve who had left the island; some had been lost in the wilds, others drowned in an attempted escape, and five the Indians had killed "for their diversions." Says the devout Vaca: "We gave many thanks at seeing ourselves together, and this was a day to us of the greatest pleasure we had enjoyed in life. . . . Thus the Almighty had been pleased to preserve me . . . that I might lead them over the bays and rivers that obstructed our progress."

Dorantes told Vaca the melancholy history of Narváez's end. He had heard it from a captive in another tribe who was presumably the sole survivor; and he had learned later that this survivor had been slain because a native woman had dreamed he was about to kill her son. Of those three hundred adventurers who had landed with

Narváez on the west coast of Florida, some the sea
had swallowed up, others had fallen prey to bitter
weather, disease, cannibalism, Indian "diversion,"
and superstition; and now but three Spaniards and
the Moor Estevanico were left alive, and these
were naked, destitute, the slaves of a fierce and
savage tribe. Vaca, on his appearance among the
two tribes at the pecan gathering, had been seized
as a slave by the cross-eyed master of Dorantes.
This was a contingency he had been prepared to
face. It was in the knowledge that the effort to escape might mean enslavement, or even death, that
Oviedo had turned back — and Vaca gone on.

Secretly the captives laid plans for their escape,
which they would postpone, however, until the
summer, when their masters would go westward to
gather prickly pears. Then "people would arrive
from parts farther on, bringing bows to barter and
for exchange, with whom, after making our escape,
we should be able to go on their return."

Summer came. On the prickly pear plains,
somewhere west of the Colorado, the captives had
made all ready for escape when their plan was
balked by an Indian quarrel. One of the factions
departed at once, taking Castillo with them. So
the Spaniards were again separated; and again

Vaca postponed his journey for another year. Next
summer the Indians would return to the prickly
pear plains and, if Castillo were still alive, then he
should find that his comrades had not abandoned
him. That Vaca himself and the two with him
might be done away with for Indian "diversion,"
or by the blasts and want of another winter, was
also a probability. But Vaca seems to have
brooded little over his own dangers. His actions
prove his words that he ever had trust that God
would lead him "out from that captivity, and thus
I always spoke of it to my companions."

Another year was passed in slavery, during
which time Vaca led a pitifully hard life. Three
times he ran away, so badly was he used, but each
time he was pursued and taken back. In September of the following year — it was now 1534 — a
third time the Spaniards met on the prickly pear
plains. Escaping at last they fled west to the Avavares, whom Vaca had met farther east when a
trader. At this village there was a sick native in
one of the tents, and his tribesmen demanded that
Vaca cure him. He restored the patient to health
and was rewarded with a supply of meat and fruit.
As the Indians told him that the country to the
westward was cold and predicted from certain

natural signs a severe winter, he counseled patience once more.

For eight months the white men continued with the Avavares, and the fame of the new Medicine Man was on every tongue. His companions were also called to the sick bed, since they might be supposed to partake of his talents. But it seems that neither Castillo nor Dorantes relished the rôle of physician. Castillo, indeed, went about his new occupation with shaking knees. He much doubted the approval of high heaven and feared, moreover, that his sins would weigh against his healing efforts. Vaca's sturdy soul knew no misgivings. He did not believe that he was dowered with mystic powers; yet he saw the sick rise up after he had blown upon them in the native fashion and made the sign of the cross over them in Christian manner. This was, to him, proof positive that God willed the preservation of himself and his friends and blessed his efforts accordingly.

When summer came (1535) the four Spaniards, turning southward, passed on to the Arbadaos. These Indians evidently lived in the great sand belt between the Nueces and the Río Grande. They were kind, but food was scarce in their desert land, and while with them the Spaniards suffered more than ever the pangs of hunger. "In the course of a whole day we did not eat more than two handfuls of fruit, which was green and contained so much milky juice that our mouths were burnt by it." In their straits they were helped out by the purchase of two dogs, for which Vaca gave the skins which covered his nakedness. He made combs, bows and arrows, nets, and the mats which formed the walls of the savages' temporary dwellings, and traded these for whatever increase of food he could get and occasionally for skins. Sometimes he was set to scraping and softening hides, and he says that the days of his "greatest prosperity" were those when he was given skins to dress, for "I would scrape them a very great deal and eat the scraps, which would sustain me for two or three days." Sometimes a piece of meat was thrown to the fugitives and they ate it raw; for, if they had put it to roast, the first native happening along would have snatched it and devoured it. Vaca remarks slyly that "it appeared to us not well to expose it to this risk."

Having consumed the dogs, the Spaniards continued their journey southward, and soon crossed a river which appeared to them to be as wide as the Guadalquivír at Seville. It was the Río Grande.

By this time the Miracle Man's fame had spread from tribe to tribe along his route. And his progress now became a triumphal march, with flocks of feathered Indians — sometimes to the number of four thousand — following in his train. His redskinned disciples greatly impeded his travel, for they all wished to touch him and his friends or some part of their clothing; and not a man of the thousands of them would eat a morsel of food until one of the Spaniards had blessed it. At the same time they hunted and dug for food along the march, killing hares, deer, opossums, gathering fruit, roots, and nuts. They never presumed to eat until they had fed their physician; nor to rest until they had erected houses for him and his three friends. Their women wove mats and blankets for the white men and made their moccasins. The natives from one village would go as far as the next; there they would proclaim to the astonished inhabitants Vaca's wondrous works, and, at the same time, plunder the village of everything worth taking. Vaca was grieved at this wholesale robbery but dared not attempt to check it. "In consolation," he says, "the plunderers told them that we were children of the sun and that we had power to heal the sick and to destroy; and other lies even greater than these, which none know how to tell better than they when they find it convenient. They bade them conduct us with great respect, advised that they should be careful to offend us in nothing, give us all they might possess, and endeavor to take us where people were numerous; and that wheresoever they arrive with us, they should rob and pillage the people of what they have, since this was customary."

The coast Indians had been hostile, but these were friendly, so the direct route to Pánuco was abandoned. Turning westward now through Coahuila, and then northward, Vaca recrossed the Río Grande west of the Pecos, struck it again at the mouth of the Conchos, and followed it to the vicinity of El Paso. And over all these leagues of wilderness the hordes of Indians continued with him. In one town Vaca performed a surgical operation with a conch-shell knife, cutting a flint arrowhead from a man's shoulder. The patient recovered; and the arrowhead was carried like a saint's relic, throughout the land, that men might marvel. From the region of El Paso, Vaca and his friends pressed westward over the arid plains of Chihuahua and crossed the Sierra Madre Mountains after many days of hard going. "The Indians," says Vaca, "ever accompanied us until they delivered us to others; and all held full faith in our coming from heaven. . . . Thus we . . . traversed all the country until coming out at the South Sea."

At a town on the Río Yaqui the Spaniards were presented with over six hundred "hearts of deer," and five arrows tipped with "emeralds" — probably malachite. This Town of the Hearts, as Vaca named it, was in the region of Sahuaripa, Sonora. Descending the Yaqui River, which empties into the Gulf of California, Vaca came upon Spaniards on a slave-hunting foray on the frontier of New Galicia. The surprise occasioned by the apparition there of these four haggard, battered, bearded, skin-clothed, paint-bedaubed Europeans can be better imagined than described. Glad indeed were the poor wanderers to see once again men of their own race, and they "gave many thanks to God our Lord."

But Vaca's feeling was not one of unmixed joy, for on every side he saw the devastation the Spaniards had wrought among the natives; half the men and all the women and boys, he says, had been carried away as slaves. The six hundred natives who had accompanied Vaca down the Yaqui offered a rich and easy prize to these slave hunters; and Vaca's urgent protests resulted only in deceitful promises. He says, "We set about to preserve the liberty of the Indians and thought we had secured it, but the contrary appeared; for the Christians had arranged to go and spring upon those we had sent away in peace and confidence. They executed their plans as they had designed."

Vaca and his comrades went on southward, through Culiacán to Compostela, then the principal town of New Galicia. Here they were hospitably received by Nuño de Guzmán, the Governor, who gave them beds, and some of his own wardrobe to screen their nakedness. But after eight years of Indian life the wanderers found that they could not wear clothes with comfort, "nor could we sleep anywhere else but on the ground."

Vaca reached the City of Mexico on July 24, 1536; thence he went to Santo Domingo, and from there to Spain. In all places his story bore fruit. In Spain he was disappointed in his ambition for the governorship of Florida. One wonders why he should have wanted it! That office had already been taken by Hernando de Soto. Vaca was invited to accompany De Soto, but his experience with Narváez had made him unwilling to take part in an expedition not commanded by himself. After three years of hopes and disappointments, Vaca was made *adelantado* of Río de la Plata, in South America. In this venture he expended all his means. In the South American wilds he made marches almost as heroic as his journey from Texas to Sonora. But his humane treatment of the natives won for him the hostility of his turbulent compatriots. He was seized, on trumped-up charges, and sent in chains to Spain. There he lay in prison for six years. He was then condemned by the Council of the Indies, stripped of his honors and titles, and sentenced to exile in Africa. Meanwhile he had become the subject of a learned controversy among clerical pamphleteers as to the propriety of a layman's performing miracles. His end is not known, though he is said to have been living in Spain twenty years later. Of his companions only the black Estevanico played a conspicuous part in later history in America. We shall hear anon how Estevanico became a permanent figure in Indian tradition.

CHAPTER III

HERNANDO DE SOTO

HERNANDO DE SOTO was about thirty-six years of age when he was appointed *adelantado* of Florida. He was "a gentleman by all four descents," and had recently been created by the Emperor a knight of the order of Santiago. He had already led a career of adventure not often equaled. He had served under Pedrarias in Nicaragua, and, by his marriage to Pedrarias's daughter, Doña Isabel, had become brother-in-law to Balboa, discoverer of the Pacific. Later, in following the fortunes of Pizarro in Peru, he had "distinguished himself over all the captains and principal personages present, not only at the seizure of Atabalipa [Atahualpa, the Inca], lord of Peru, and in carrying the City of Cuzco, but at all other places wheresoever he went and found resistance." Thus does the Gentleman of Elvas, comrade of Don Hernando and narrator of his exploits, pen his biography in a line. A man of blood

46

and iron, wherever he "found resistance" there Hernando de Soto was roused to action. He brooked neither opposition from foes nor interference from friends; and, for him, no peril, no hardship, could surpass in bitterness the defeat of his will. His nature was to be read plainly in his swarthy, strongly lined face and burning black eyes, and in the proud carriage of his head; so that, though he was hardly more than of medium stature, men remarked him and gave him room. He had an agreeable smile at rare moments; he was renowned for courage, and his skill as a horseman was noted among those lovers of horses, the Spanish nobles. He was able to set up a fine establishment and to lend money to the Emperor Charles V, from whom he was seeking high office. And so the Emperor made him Governor of Cuba and *adelantado* of Florida. Narváez had pictured in Florida another Mexico. De Soto hoped to find there another Peru.

The news of De Soto's expedition took his countrymen by storm. When Vaca, fresh from his wanderings, appeared at court and told his great tale, the enthusiasm increased. Rich nobles sold their estates, their houses, vineyards, and olive-fields, their plate and jewels, their towns of vassals, to participate in the venture. There assembled in Seville so many "persons of noble extraction" that a large number of those who had sold all they had were forced to remain behind for want of shipping. De Soto mustered his volunteers for review at the port of Sanlúcar. Here he scanned them carefully and picked out his men, who were then counted and enlisted. They numbered six hundred. And, considering the small size of the ships of that day, they and their supplies must have been tightly packed in the nine vessels that bore them from Spain.

On Sunday morning of the day of St. Lazarus, April, 1538, Hernando de Soto in a "new ship fast of sail" led his fleet over the bar of Sanlúcar, "with great festivity." From every vessel artillery roared at his command, and trumpets sounded. Favorable winds urged his vessels on; his adored Doña Isabel was beside him, adventure and fame were before him.

On Pentecost Day the ships were moored in the harbor of Santiago de Cuba. All the horsemen and footmen of the town surged down to the landing; and Don Hernando and Doña Isabel, followed by their train of six hundred, rode into the city, where they were "well lodged, attentively visited, and

served by all the citizens." From Santiago Don
Hernando sent Doña Isabel and the ships to Havana, his port of embarkment for Florida; while
with one hundred and fifty horsemen he made a
tour of the cities under his authority. Presently
he heard that his ships bound for Havana had experienced severe storms, which had swept them out
of their course and separated them. But after
forty days they had all come safely to Havana.
Leaving his cavalcade to follow as it might, Don
Hernando mounted and made all speed to Havana
and Doña Isabel.

On Sunday, May 18, 1539, De Soto said farewell
to his wife and sailed from Havana for Florida, the
land still reputed to be "the richest of any which
until then had been discovered"; and on the thirtieth he landed his men near an Indian town on
Tampa Bay. Here the Spaniards immediately had
a brush with the natives, who let drive at the armored horsemen with their arrows. Two savages
were killed; the others fled through wooded and
boggy country where the horses could not follow.
And, when the Spaniards lay in camp that night
they could see flames come out against the blackness, dwindling in the distance to specks like fire-
flies, as the Indians passed their fiery warning

inland. Two days later they came upon a deserted town of eight huts. De Soto established headquarters there and sent out several companies of horse and foot to explore. He ordered the woods felled "the distance of a crossbow shot" around the town. He set sentinels about the place and detailed horsemen to go the rounds. After having made all secure, he lodged himself in the chief's house. And there, in the dust flooring, under his torch's glare, he found a small scatter of pearls. They were ruined by the fire used in boring them for beads; but to him they were typical of the jewelled chain of fortune which should link him with greatness to his life's end and as long after as men's tongues should wag. So had Narváez thought when he found the golden ornament.

When the exploring parties returned they could relate that the Indians of Florida were no mean foes. One party brought back six men wounded — one so badly that he died. But they had captured four women. Another party brought in a man — a white man. This was Juan Ortiz, of noble lineage, follower of the fortunes of Narváez, and for the last eleven years a slave among the savages. He had entered Florida with Narváez, but instead of following his leader inland, had stuck to the ships and had returned to Cuba. Then Narváez's wife had sent him back to Florida in a pinnace to look for her husband, and there he had been taken captive. An Indian girl, he said — apparently a prototype of Pocahontas — had romantically saved his life, just as he was about to be roasted alive at the command of her father. In passing from tribe to tribe, sometimes in barter, sometimes as a fugitive, Ortiz had become conversant with several dialects and he could now play the rôle of interpreter. To De Soto's eager inquiries he answered that he had seen no gold nor jewels, but had heard of a rich country thirty leagues inland. This was enough. De Soto now dispatched his ships to Cuba for more supplies and ordered his company to make ready to march.

This was the beginning of three years of restless wandering, in the course of which De Soto and his men traversed Florida, Georgia, Carolina, Tennessee, Alabama, Mississippi, Arkansas, Oklahoma, Louisiana, and Texas.

Leaving at the camp a garrison of fifty footmen with thirty horses and food for two years, on August 1, 1539, De Soto set out. In his train were some five hundred and fifty lancers, crossbowmen, and arquebusiers, about two hundred horses, a number of priests and Dominican friars — with the sacred vessels, vestments, and white meal for the Mass; a physician and his medicines; a ship's carpenter, calkers, and a cooper for the boat-building that might be necessary on inland waters — perhaps to construct a ship to bear Don Hernando to China by that fabled waterway Columbus had not found. And there were armorers and smiths, with their forges and tools, for mail shirts must be mended betimes, swords tempered, and the great bulk of iron chains and iron slave-collars kept in good repair.

They were bound northwestward to the country of Cale. Indians had told them that beyond Cale, "towards the sunset," lay a land of perpetual summer where there was so much gold that, when its people came down to war with the tribes of Cale, "they wore golden hats like casques."

On towards that land of golden hats went the Spaniards; over low thicketed country full of bogs and swamps, where the horses, weighted by their own armor and their heavily accoutered riders, mired and floundered. They crossed several small rivers on logs, swimming the horses over by a hawser. This was not the country, "very rich in maize," which Indians had told them stretched along the way to Cale. Pinched by hunger, the

Spaniards ate young palm shoots and water cresses
"without other thing." And, from the thickets
about the bogs and marshes, invisible savages sent
a rain of arrows upon them.

"He came to Cale and found the town abandoned," tersely writes the Gentleman of Elvas
Cale was a huddle of mud and palmetto huts some
where on the Suwanee River. But there was ripe
maize in the Indian fields, enough to supply De
Soto's men for three months; three men were killed
during the husking. The Indians kept under cover,
and no slaves could be taken; so the Spaniards were
forced to grind their own corn for bread. Some of
them ground it in the log mortars they found in the
town and sifted the flour through their mail shirts.
The majority, disdaining this menial toil, ate the
grains "parched and sodden."

No golden hats were found in Cale, so De Soto
pushed on northwestward to Caliquen. Along his
route he set a company of his horsemen and a pack
of greyhounds sharply to work catching Indians.
For an army in a strange land needed guides; and
gentlemen unskilled in bread-making needed slaves.
Like Cortés he made a practice of seizing the chief
of each town on his march — after an exchange of
compliments and fraternal testimonials. Then he

held him to insure the tribe's peaceful conduct; and forced him to supply food and men and women for the use of the army.

De Soto's first pitched battle with the Indians resulted from an attempt made by the natives of Caliquen to rescue their chief. Ortiz, who knew their language, informed him of the plot. Four hundred natives stationed themselves outside the camp and sent two of their number to demand their chief's release. De Soto took the chief by the hand and led him out, accompanied by a dozen foot soldiers; and then, having thrown the Indians off guard by this strategy, he ordered the trumpet sounded. Shouting their battle cry of "Santiago" the Spaniards bore down upon the Indians, and, after a brief fierce fight, routed them and killed from thirty to forty, while the rest leaped into two nearby lakes to escape the horsemen's lances. The Spaniards surrounded one of the lakes; and during the night some, more alert-eyed than others, observed the odd phenomenon of water-lilies slowly moving inshore over the moonlit surface of the water. The Indians had put the lilies on their heads and were swimming noiselessly and with barely a ripple towards land. The Spaniards rushed in, to their horses' breasts, and drove them back. The next day all but a few were captured and divided among the Spaniards as slaves. The forges were in full blast that day for the riveting of chains and iron collars.

But, though chained, the natives of Caliquen were not tamed. They rose against their captors, seized their weapons, and, whether lances or swords, handled them as if accustomed to use them all their lives; so says the Gentleman of Elvas, who took part in the mêlée. "One Indian, in the public yard of the town, with blade in hand, fought like a bull in the arena, until the halberdiers of the Governor, arriving, put an end to him."

A further march of about thirty miles brought the Spaniards to a town of the Appalachees near Tallahassee, probably the same visited by Narváez. There they found the October fields of grain, beans, and pumpkins ready to harvest, and decided to go into camp for the winter. From this point De Soto dispatched communications to his ships at Tampa and sent letters, with a present of twenty Indian women captives, to be carried to Doña Isabel in Cuba. The army remained in camp till March.

Besides the men sent to the ships at Tampa Bay -- who were to bring back the garrison left there — De Soto sent out two exploring parties. One of these parties discovered Pensacola Bay. The other came suddenly upon a beautiful bay at no great distance from the camp. Its blue waves, with the amethystine streak characteristic of Southern waters, were vivid under the sun, which smote to glistening scattered white objects like little heaps of pearl along its shore. This bay was the Bay of Horses, whence Narváez and his men had set out in their horsehide boats. The glistening white heaps were the bleached bones and skulls of their slain mounts.

Besought by his men "to leave the land of Florida," lest they all perish like Narváez, De Soto sternly replied that he would never turn back. In his heart he had already resolved to go on until he should find the golden country he sought; or, failing in that search, to perish rather than return to bear the chagrin of seeing himself outdone by some other conquistador who, by greater perseverance, might discover "another Mexico" in the great interior.

So, on March 3, 1540, De Soto broke camp and took his way northeastward, across the present State of Georgia, through the country of the Creeks. Towards the end of April he reached a town called Cufitachiqui. It was on the Savannah River.

probably somewhere below Augusta; Indian tradition locates it at the modern Silver Bluff. The cacica, or chieftainess, richly draped in furs and feathers, with loops of pearls depending from her neck, crossed the river in a canoe to greet Don Hernando, accompanied by her men of state and followed by a fleet of canoes laden with gifts for the visiting prince. After speeches of welcome, she took off a large string of pearls and threw it about De Soto's neck. Then she offered more canoes brought to convey him and his men to the other side. Seeing that the pearls rejoiced him, she told him that if he would open the burial mounds he would find many more and that, in some deserted towns nearby, "he might load all his horses with them." So from the graves at Cufitachiqui De Soto took three hundred and fifty pounds of pearls "and figures of babies and birds made of them." He found also a dirk and some rosaries that had once belonged to Ayllón's followers.

At Cufitachiqui De Soto's men desired to make a settlement. It was a favorable point to begin colonization. It lay but two days' journey from the sea "to which could come all the ships from New Spain"; and it was "a good country, and one fit in which to raise supplies." But De Soto was

looking for another treasure such as he had wrested
from the Inca in Peru and he "would not be content with good lands nor pearls," saying that
"should a richer country not be found, they could
always return to that who would."   He then asked
the cacica if there were "any great lord farther on"
and was blandly told of the rich province of Chiaha,
subject to a chief of Coosa. To seek this new goal
he resolved to go at once, and "being an inflexible
man, and dry of word, who, although he liked to
know what the others all thought and had to say,
after he once said a thing he did not like to be opposed, and as he ever acted as he thought best, all
bent to his will . . . there were none who would
say a thing to him after it became known that he
had made up his mind."   It was discovered presently that this red-skinned Cleopatra now wished
to slip away from her Antony, and without giving him carriers for his supplies, "because of the
outrages committed upon the inhabitants."   So
De Soto put her under guard and carried her away
on foot with her female slaves. This treatment,
as the Gentleman of Elvas remarks, "was not a
proper return" for the hospitality and affectionate
welcome he had received.

Seven days' marching brought the Spaniards

into the country of the Cherokees; and five days later they reached Xualla, a Cherokee town above the junction of the Tuckaseegee and Oconna-Luftee rivers in Swain County, North Carolina. On the way the cacica of Cufitachiqui had escaped; and — more untimely loss — had carried into the thickets with her "a cane box, like a trunk," full of unbored pearls. "And the Governor, not to give offense, permitted it so, thinking that in Guaxulle he would beg them of her when he should give her leave to depart." Still pushing on towards that "richest province," De Soto crossed the Smoky Mountains and went into Tennessee. He tarried at Guaxule, where the chief's house stood on a great mound, surrounded by a terrace on which half a dozen men could walk abreast. Here he was fortunate enough to get three hundred "dogs" — perhaps opossums — as meat for his army. But this hilly country was unprofitable to man and beast. De Soto therefore turned south into Georgia, to see that "greatest prince" of Coosa. There was no lack of food as he pressed on southward; for the natives willingly contributed mulberries, nuts, maize, and wild turkeys.

De Soto's course took him down the Coosa River to Chiaha, a town of the Creeks. Coosa,

in Talladega County, Alabama, where men and
beasts waxed fat on the abundance of the land, was
reached on the 26th of July. Remembrance of
Coosa lingered with these Spaniards and lured
some of them back in after years. The chief of
Coosa, arrayed in a wonderful shawl of marten
skins — in mid-July, and in Alabama! — and preceded by men playing upon small flutes, came out
to meet De Soto and invited him to settle in his
country. But De Soto was not interested in furs,
and he saw no gold in Coosa. So, after having
seized a number of slaves and the chief himself, he
went on, southward now, through Alabama. Near
the Alabama River he was shown another gloomy
memento of Spanish adventurers in that land. This
was the dagger of Theodoro, the Greek, who had
come ashore at the river's mouth to get fresh water
for Narváez's men some eleven years before.

On the 15th of October, having crossed the Alabama, De Soto reached Mavilla, a large town near
the present Choctaw Bluff. The name Mavilla is
preserved in that of Mobile, city and river. At
Mavilla was fought the fiercest combat of the entire march. The Indians soon set upon the Spaniards and drove them outside the walls of the town.
They seized all the baggage, including provisions,

some arms, and the three hundred and fifty pounds of pearls, gathered in the slaves, struck off their chains and armed them. De Soto drew up his army and made a fierce assault upon the stockade, while, within one of the houses, some soldiers, a priest, and a friar, who had been trapped there, fought off the Indians at the door with swords and clubs. De Soto ordered the town fired; and, as the flames burst forth from the roofs and the natives attempted to flee, he broke through with his soldiery and took possession. Eighteen Spaniards and twelve horses were killed, and one hundred and fifty Spaniards and seventy horses were badly wounded with arrows. The Indians were slaughtered almost to a man; for, as they attempted to flee, the Spanish horsemen drove them back into the burning town. There, "losing the hope of escape, they fought valiantly; and the Christians getting among them with cutlasses, they found themselves met on all sides by their strokes, when many, dashing into the flaming houses, were smothered, and, heaped one upon another, burned to death. . . . The struggle lasted so long that many Christians, weary and very thirsty, went to drink at a pond nearby, tinged with the blood of the killed." In the fire were consumed all the

baggage and supplies, the pearls, and the vessels
for the Mass.

Now De Soto, himself severely wounded, — for
always he led his men when he ordered an attack,
— heard that at the coast, six days distant, ships
from Cuba commanded by his lieutenant, Maldonado, rode at anchor waiting for news of him and
bearing supplies for the army, as well as letters
from Doña Isabel. But he ordered that this information be kept from his men, who were already
disillusioned about golden Florida and eager to
leave it. The pearls which he had intended to send
to Cuba "for show, that their fame might raise the
desire of coming to Florida," had been destroyed;
and as he feared the effect of sending word of himself without "either gold or silver, or other thing
of value," he determined to send no news of
himself until he should have discovered a rich
country. So the ships waited their appointed
time, and then sailed home again, bearing to Cuba
no word of its Governor, and to Doña Isabel
only silence.

At the time of his decision De Soto's force was
lessened by one hundred and two men, who had
been slain or lost on his long march; the remainder
were in tatters, or naked, under their rusty mail;

many of his horses, all his supplies and extra clothing, and his slim booty were destroyed; and his men no longer shared what little hope may have remained to him of ever reaching that richest province "beyond."   But if his decision, made for his pride and his honor and against the love of his wife and his own chances of survival, cost him anything, no hint of that cost passed his stern lips. For twenty-eight days he rested at Mavilla to allow the wounded, who dressed their wounds with the fat of the slain Indians, to recover; then he took up the search again.

On the 17th of November De Soto moved northwestward in quest of another Promised Land, a place called Pacaha.   He crossed the Black Warrior and the Tombigbee rivers and a month later entered a Chickasaw town in the present State of Mississippi, where he went into winter quarters. Before spring he had his troubles with the proud and warlike Chickasaws.   Some of the natives, caught in theft, were executed; and another, "his hands having first been cut off," was sent back to the chief as a visible warning.   Four Spaniards, who pillaged some Indian houses, almost met with as hard a fate; for De Soto, stern with friend and foe alike, ordered two of them put to death and the

other two deprived of their goods. Deaf to all
pleas, he would have seen the sentence carried
out but for the subtlety of Ortiz, the interpreter,
who translated the complaints of the Indians into
prayers for pardon.

When, in March, De Soto was ready to depart,
he made his usual demand for male carriers and for
women. The Chickasaws considered this an in-
sult to be wiped out in blood. They fell upon the
Spaniards at dawn; and, "by the time those in the
town were aware, half the houses were in flames."
The men, running in confusion from the fire,
blinded by the smoke and the glare, not able to find
their arms nor to saddle their horses, fell easy prey
to the native archers. The horses snapped their
halters and stampeded, or were burned to death in
their stalls. It would have been a complete victory
for the Indians — and the end of the expedition —
if the natives had not believed that the thunder of
hoofs meant that the cavalry was gathering to fall
upon them. They fled, leaving only one dead on
the field. He had been killed with a lance by De
Soto, who was unhorsed in the act because his
saddle girth was loose. Eleven Spaniards and fifty
horses perished. The army then quickly moved to
another town and turned to at making saddles and

lances from ash, and grass mats, to protect their
naked bodies from the cold. Towards the end of
April, De Soto started on, northwestward, and,
during the first week in May, 1541, not far from
the Chickasaw Bluffs, he stood on the east bank of
the Mississippi River.

On the plains, a crossbow's shot from the steep
timbered bank, the army pitched camp. De Soto
set his men at once to felling trees and constructing
vessels in which to cross the river; for on the west
shore to the north, lay the "richest province" of
Pacaha, whither he was bound. Presently the
cacique of Aquixo, or Arkansas, came over to visit
him, with his lesser chiefs and two hundred warriors. The chiefs sat in the sterns of their canoes
under skin awnings; and chiefs and warriors were
"painted with ochre, wearing great bunches of
white and other plumes of many colors." Some
held "feathered shields in their hands, with which
they sheltered the oarsmen on either side, the warriors standing erect from bow to stern, holding
bows and arrows. . . . These were fine-looking
men, very large and well-formed; and what with
the awnings, the plumes, and the shields, the pen-
nons, and the number of people in the fleet, it appeared like a famous armada of galleys." The

5

canoes also bore gifts of furs, buffalo robes, dried fruits, and fish for the white chief. These the cacique sent ashore; but when De Soto and his men came down to the water's edge, making signs to him to land, he hastily ordered his oarsmen to retreat, evidently in apprehension of the strange men in armor the like of which he had never seen before. De Soto, construing this as hostility, ordered the crossbowmen to fire. Half a dozen Indians fell; but the canoes continued to retire in good order, not an Indian "leaving the oar, even though the one next to him might have fallen." During the month consumed in barge-building, the Indians appeared in midstream several times but came no nearer. Early one June morning the barges were passing to and fro across the Mississippi; and by sunrise all the men and horses were on the west bank The barges were then taken to pieces and the iron spikes were kept for making other vessels when needed.

Marching north through Arkansas, from some captives now De Soto heard more of Chisca, beyond Pacaha, where there was much gold. He found the towns along his route deserted. The inhabitants had fled and hidden themselves; but the Spaniards felt their presence in the arrow flights which descended on them from the ravines and thick timber, as they paused to find the best crossings over streams and marshes. After crossing Fifteen-Mile Bayou in St. Francis County, Arkansas, they marched all day until sunset over flooded ground. The water was sometimes as high as their waists. At night they reached Casqui, "where they found the Indians off their guard, never having heard of them." They seized all the buffalo robes and furs in the town and many of the men and women. The towns here were thickly set in a very fruitful country; so that, while the footmen were despoiling one town, the horsemen could sweep down upon another. De Soto made friends with the chief of Casqui, who was on bad terms with the chief of Pacaha, and set up a cross in his town. After having "pacified" Pacaha, De Soto reconciled its chief to the chief of Casqui and entertained both worthies at dinner. Whereupon the chief of Casqui gave De Soto his daughter to wife; and the chief of Pacaha, by an equally simple marriage ceremony, gave him two of his sisters, Macanoche and Mochila. Of the Pacaha ladies the discriminating Gentleman of Elvas says: "They were symmetrical, tall, and full; Macanoche bore a pleasant expression; in her manners and features appeared the lady; the other was robust."

Again it was the same old story. No gold was found at Pacaha; but, at Caluça "beyond," there was said to be some. So eighty men were sent out to look over Caluça and to discover the best road to Chisca, where there was gold in plenty and a copper foundry! We can only conjecture as to what the Indians were trying to tell De Soto when he visualized, from their signs, a copper foundry. When his party of explorers returned after a week's journey northward across Missouri, they could report no gold, but they had heard of the great buffalo-covered prairies beyond. In their wanderings they had perhaps reached the Osage, or even the Kansas.

These dispiriting reports determined Don Hernando not to seek for Chisca and its fabled gold. After a rest of some weeks in Pacaha he moved westward across northern Arkansas to the abundant grain fields of Tanico, probably on the Neosho River in Oklahoma. Here he halted for a month to garner supplies and fatten his horses. From Tanico he turned southeastward. He crossed the Arkansas in the vicinity of Fort Smith on the dividing line between Oklahoma and Arkansas, and went into winter quarters about thirty miles east of the line at an Indian town named Autiamque on the south bank of the Arkansas River. Here the Spaniards spent three months, during one of which snow fell almost continuously. The shackled Indians built a high palisade about the camp, hauled wood for fires, and trapped rabbits for food. Juan Ortiz, the castaway of Narváez's expedition, died at Autiamque; and, as he was the only man with a fair knowledge of Indian speech, his loss was a serious blow to De Soto's army.

Spring came, and in March, 1542, De Soto broke camp and continued down the Arkansas. By this time, of the six hundred who had come with him from Spain "he had not over three hundred efficient men, nor more than forty horses. Some of the beasts were lame, and useful only in making out the show of a troop of cavalry; and, for the lack of iron, they had gone a year without shoes." De Soto resolved now to go to the seacoast, which he imagined to be not far off. There he would build two vessels, one to be sent to New Spain and the other to Cuba, "calculating, out of his property there, to refit and again go back to advance, to discover and to conquer farther on towards the west." It was three years since he had been heard of by Doña Isabel, nor did he know how she fared. In April he reached Guachoya, at the mouth of the Arkansas, and, as usual, lodged his men in the town, from which most of the natives had fled at his approach. To ascertain how near the sea was, he sent several men down the Mississippi, but when they returned after more than a week's absence it was to tell him that only the river's tide, to bayous and swamps, stretched for miles upon miles below. Nor could the Indians they had captured down the river tell them of any other great water.

No news of the sea — and men and horses dying off; his little company ringed round with hostile tribes, whom he had treated without mercy in the days of his strength; and no succor anywhere; "of that reflection he pined." At the recognition, at last, of defeat the strong spirit of Don Hernando broke and his body weakened under the fever of torment that took hold of him. But still he had nerve. From his straw pallet he dispatched a messenger commanding the chief of Quigaltam across the river to send him carriers and provisions; for he was the "Child of the Sun," and "whence he came all obeyed him, rendering their tribute." The chief returned answer that the Child of the Sun should be able to dry up the river between them. On that token, he would believe. "If you desire to see me come where I am . . .

neither for you nor for any man, will I set back one foot."

Here, at last, by his words, was the "greatest prince" so long sought. De Soto was already low by the time his messenger returned; but, on hearing the chief's insolent answer, his haughty spirit blazed up once more and he grieved that there was not bodily force left in him to enable him to cross the river and abate that pride. As an object-lesson not alone to the lofty cacique but also to the Indians of Guachoya, whose treachery he feared, he sent an expedition to lay waste and slaughter the town of Nilco some distance off. The Spaniards took the inhabitants so entirely by surprise that, when the captain ordered all males slain, not an Indian was ready to draw his bow in defense. "The cries of the women and children were such as to deafen those who pursued them. About one hundred men were slain; many were allowed to get away badly wounded that they might strike terror into those who were absent. Some persons were so cruel and butcher-like that they killed all before them, young and old, not one having resisted little or much." If the Indians of Guachoya had indeed been planning an attack, the object lesson had the desired effect.

De Soto's hour had struck, and he lay dying in loneliness. His officers and men, gloomy over their own prospects and resentful against the commander who had led them to this pass, held aloof — "each one himself having need of sympathy, which was the cause why they neither gave him their companionship nor visited him." On the day before his death he called for them. After giving thanks to God, he confessed his deep obligations to them all "for their great qualities, their love and loyalty to his person"; and he asked their prayers and their forgiveness of any wrongs that he might have dealt them. And, to prevent divisions, he requested them to elect his successor, saying "that this would greatly satisfy him, abate somewhat the pains he suffered, and moderate the anxiety of leaving them in a country, they knew not where." One officer responded in behalf of all, "consoling him with remarks on the shortness of the life of this world," and with many other high-sounding cold phrases; and requested the Governor himself to select their new leader. De Soto chose Luís de Moscoso; and the others willingly swore to obey him.

On the morrow, the 21st of May, having made his last will and his last confession, "departed this life the magnanimous, the virtuous, the intrepid captain, Don Hernando de Soto, Governor of Cuba and *adelantado* of Florida.   He was advanced by fortune, in the way she is wont to lead others, that he might fall the greater depth."

The death of the Child of the Sun was kept secret from the Indians, from fear of an uprising. His body was buried at night just within the walls of the town and the Indians were told that he had ascended to the Sun; but the natives observed that the earth near the wall had been disturbed and were seen talking among themselves. So, as secretly as it had been buried, De Soto's body was dug up. A safer grave must be found for it — a grave safer to the living. Packed with sand to weight it down, and the mass wrapped and closely bound in "shawls," it was taken out in a canoe to midstream, and there under the blackness of the night — with no sound save a whispered order and one deep answering note from the waters — it sank into the river.

What were these "shawls," fashioned into a winding-sheet for the man who had hungered for riches and died empty of them? Were they the mantles of marten, deer, and beaver skins the Indians wore and which the Spaniards so little esteemed? Everywhere about De Soto, on his past marches through that great fur-bearing country, lay the "richest province" he sought; and already, far to the north, the codfishers of France on the Newfoundland Banks were carrying home furs to trade in the markets of St. Malo and Rouen. There is the irony of tragedy in the picture of the intrepid gold-hunter's body consigned to the keeping of the Father of Waters shrouded in furs — which were to constitute the great wealth of this continent for more than two hundred years. On the broad flood of the Mississippi, flowing over De Soto's last resting place, were to pass the canoes and the pirogues of the fur traders, laden with the packs of peltry which should turn to gold in the French and English markets.

The *adelantado* had fallen, but the wanderings of his followers were by no means over. "Some were glad of the death of Don Hernando de Soto, holding it certain that Luís de Moscoso, who was given to leading a gay life, preferred to see himself at ease in a land of Christians, rather than continue the toils of war, discovering and subduing, which the people had come to hate, finding the little recompense that followed." After consultation with

his officers, Moscoso decided to try to reach Mexico
by land. On the 5th of June the Spaniards moved
westward, headed for Pánuco. They crossed
southern Arkansas and reached the Red River near
Texarkana, but were prevented for a week by a
flood from crossing the river. Their march dupli-
cated many past events, in battles with Indians,
in slave-catching raids, and ambushes. At the
Red River they changed their course to the south
and entered the Caddo villages of eastern Texas;
then, veering southwest again, they came to a large
river, probably the middle Brazos. Here, as in
Missouri and Oklahoma, they heard of the buffalo
plains beyond, but did not reach them. October
had come, winter was on the way, and the country promised little succor through the cold and
snow. So they turned back on their trail to one
of the villages on the Mississippi near the mouth
of the Arkansas, where De Soto had died.

They now resolved to descend the Great River,
which must somewhere empty into the sea. In
order to do so they must build a fleet of brigantines,
capable of weathering the winds and billows of the
ocean. And now Moscoso performed a feat in shipbuilding, parallel to that of Narváez at the Bay of
Horses. At his orders timber was felled; a forge

was set up, and iron chains converted into spikes.
A Portuguese who had learned to saw lumber while
a captive in Morocco, and who had brought saws
with him, cut the planks and taught other men to
help him. A Genoese, the only man "who knew
how to construct vessels," built the brigantines
with the help of four or five Biscayan carpenters;
and two calkers, one a Genoese, the other a Sardin-
ian, closed up the cracks with "the oakum, got
from a plant like hemp, called enequen." A cooper,
who was so ill that he could barely get about, managed nevertheless to make for each of the seven
ships two half-hogsheads to hold fresh water. Sails
were made of woven hemp and skins; ropes and
cables from mulberry bark; and anchors from
stirrups. In June the brigantines were finished,
and the high floods floated them off the building
ground into the river; fortunately, for if they had
been dragged down the bank "there would have
been danger of tearing open the bottoms, thereby
entirely wrecking them, the planks being thin,
and the spikes made short for the lack of iron."
Twenty-two horses were taken aboard; the others,
being done for as mounts, were killed and their flesh
was served.

On July 3, 1543, the three hundred and twenty

Spaniards and one hundred Indian slaves set sail
for their unknown port. The rest of the captives
had been released. Savages along their course
several times beset the vessels, and ten Spaniards
were slain. Seventeen days after their departure
from the mouth of the Arkansas they reached the
sea. At first they sailed westward, following the
shore line, then steered for the open but turned in
again to the coast, thinking their frail vessel safer
within hail of the shore. They experienced hunger
and thirst, doubts and fears, and storms of the sea.
Fierce head winds forced them, at one time, to
spend fourteen days in a sheltered inlet on the Texas
coast. On the day when again it blew fair for
them, they "very devoutly formed a procession for
the return of thanks," and as they moved along
the beach they supplicated the Almighty to take
them to a land in which they might better do
Him service.

On September 10, 1543, two months and seven
days after launching their brigantines, they entered
the mouth of the Pánuco River, which flows into
the Gulf one hundred and fifty miles north of Vera
Cruz. It waters the Tampico region, today made
golden by its output of petroleum. But of oil
Moscoso neither knew nor cared. Here Indians

"in the apparel of Spain" told them in their own
tongue that there was a Christian town fifteen
leagues inland; "they felt as though life had been
newly given them; many, leaping on shore, kissed
the ground; and, all on bended knees, with hands
raised above them, and their eyes to heaven, remained untiring in giving thanks to God." Weather-
beaten and toil-worn, they entered the town, each
man clad in deerskins "dressed and dyed black"
and carrying his pack on his back; and all went
directly to the church to return thanks for their
preservation and to take part "in the divine offices
which for a long season had not been listened to
by them." The three hundred and ten men were
warmly received by their countrymen and treated
to the best the country provided.

In October, that Maldonado who had waited in
vain at Pensacola Bay to deliver to Don Hernando
Doña Isabel's letters and had twice since sought
for him along the Florida coast, arrived at Vera
Cruz. And he bore back to Cuba the news of Don
Hernando's fate. When Doña Isabel learned of
her husband's death she withered under the blow
and died within a few days. And there was no man
now in the Spanish islands who desired to tempt
heaven in the barren land of Florida.

CHAPTER IV

CORONADO, CABRILLO, AND VIZCAÍNO

MEANWHILE other Spanish explorers were trying to pierce the Northern Mystery by way of the Pacific slope.

West as well as east, and somewhere in the north, must lie the waters of the Strait of Anian, that direct passage from the Atlantic to China, if indeed the northwestern territory did not actually abut on Asia. So reasoned the Spanish dons. To the northwest, some said, was an island inhabited solely by giantesque Amazons. Inland were the Seven Cities, situated on a great height. Their doors were studded with turquoises, as if feathers from the wings of the blue sky had dropped and clung there. Within those jeweled cities were whole streets of goldsmiths, so great was the store of shining metal to be worked.

Indians were ever great story-tellers, delighting to weave the tales most pleasant to their hearers.

It was an Indian slave of Nuño de Guzmán who regaled that credulous official of New Spain with fanciful description of the Pueblo towns of New Mexico. The myth led Guzmán north, to the ruthless conquest of Sinaloa and the founding of Culiacán, still the capital city of that Mexican state.

Then, in 1535, came Antonio de Mendoza from Old Spain to be the first Viceroy of New Spain. Mendoza had soon set his heart on the acquisition of those Seven Cities. The arrival of Vaca and his companions in the City of Mexico, out of the mysterious north, in July, 1536, added fuel to Mendoza's desires. An expedition must be fitted out immediately, to be led by Vaca's companion Dorantes — since Vaca himself was resolved to go to Spain. This plan came to nothing for the time being, but Vaca left the Moor Estevanico to serve Mendoza.

Three years passed before Mendoza could prepare another expedition. Francisco Vásquez de Coronado was then (1539) made Governor of New Galicia and military head of the force designed to spread the power of Spain northward. To the Franciscan Fray Marcos de Niza was given the spiritual leadership of the expedition. Fray Marcos had already seen strenuous service, for he had been with Pizarro in the conquest of Peru. He had also written several works about the country. He had high acquirements in theology, cosmography, and navigation; and he was a hardy traveler, having tramped from Guatemala to Mexico.

To Culiacán Fray Marcos and Coronado journeyed in company. Coronado there halted to establish his authority over the outposts of New Galicia. Fray Marcos, with the Moor Estevanico, some Mexican Indians, and a few other natives who had come with Vaca's little band to Mexico, went on. Estevanico, having wandered through parts of the northern land with Vaca, was relied upon not alone to guide the friars but to insure the friendship of the Indians.

At Vacapa, somewhere in Sonora, Fray Marcos paused and, "on Passion Sunday after dinner," sent Estevanico ahead to learn what he could. Should Estevanico hear tidings of but a fair country he was to send to the friar a small cross; for great tidings, a cross "two handfuls long"; and, should he discover a country richer than Mexico, he was to send a great cross. Imagine the pleasureable agitation in the friar's breast, when, four days later, some of the Indians who had gone with the Moor came in bearing a cross "as high as a man" and a message urging Fray Marcos to follow at once. Estevanico had found a new people, who had told him of "the greatest thing in the world." He was now at a town but thirty days' journey from the turquoise doors of the Seven Cities which, he had learned, were called Cíbola; and beyond Cíbola there were other rich provinces, each one of which was "a much greater matter than those seven cities." So, as ever in these tales, the splendor within reach was already dimmed by the splendor beyond! To Cíbola,[1] therefore, the friar set out on the second day after Easter.

He is supposed to have gone directly north up the Sonora valley, though it may have been the Yaqui valley. As he went, from time to time he planted crosses; for "it appeared to me suitable from here on to perform acts of possession." He heard from the Indians on his route more details of Cíbola and of the cities beyond. And he was much surprised to learn that the natives of those

[1] Cíbola is believed to be a Spanish form of the word *Shiwina*, by which the Zuñi called their tribal range. The Spaniards later called the buffalo Cíbola. It is customary for writers to state that Guzmán and Fray Marcos set out to find the Seven Cities of Cíbola, but it was not till Estevanico sent back his report that the name Cíbola was known to the Spaniards.

cities dressed in habits of gray wool like his own.
These were perhaps the blanket garments made of
narrow strips of rabbit fur and yucca fiber which
are still woven by the Moqui Indians.   Through
the valley of the San Pedro in Arizona Fray Marcos
continued northward; then, finding that the stream
led him too far west, he veered to the northeast
and reached the Gila, above its confluence with the
San Pedro.   Here he learned that Estevanico, with
three hundred Indians, was crossing the plains to
the northeast, where the Apaches now have their
reservation.   After a rest, on May 9, 1539, Fray
Marcos continued his march to Cíbola, which lay
fifteen days beyond.   His way now led upward,
through rugged country, to a pass not identified,
between the Sierra Mogoyon and Sierra Blanca
ranges.   Bad news met him on the Apache plains.
An Indian of the Moor's escort, returning in flight,
told him that Estevanico had been seized and made
prisoner by the natives of Cíbola.

We know very little about the end of Estevanico,
this African who was one of the earliest explorers of
North America and had wandered over a greater
part of its wilderness than any man before him or
than any man for long after him.   The Arab was
one of a fearless race, loving freedom no doubt as

his tribesmen of the Moroccan deserts today love
it; and only in the desert could he enjoy it.   Lifted
again out of the thrall of slavery, which had fastened on him after his great journey from Florida,
and given command of some three hundred savages
to discover the cities of argent traceries and turquoise doors, he had made his tour like an Oriental chieftain, or like a Moorish prince before the
Conquest, with pomp and display and the revels
of power.   Gifts were brought him and tribute was
exacted.   His tall, dusky body soon flaunted robes
dyed with the colors of the rainbow.   Tufts of
brilliant feathers and strings of bells dangled from
his arms and legs.   He carried a magical gourd,
decorated with bells and with one white and one
scarlet feather; and sent it ahead of him to awe
the natives in each town where he demanded en-
trance.   A score, perhaps, of Indians formed his
personal retinue and bore on their shoulders the
provisions, the turquoises, mantles, and feathered
ornaments accumulated on the road.   Flutes of
reeds, shell fifes, and fish-skin drums played his
march across the sunlit mesas.   And an ever increasing harem of gayly bedecked young women
swelled the parade of Estevanico, the black Berber
chief, on his way to the city set in silver and blue.

Perhaps, as has been suggested, the belled and feathered gourd was "bad medicine" to the Indians of Hawikuh; for, when Estevanico's messenger presented it with the announcement that their lord was come to make peace and to cure the sick, the Indians became enraged and ordered the interlopers out of their country on pain of death. Estevanico, disdaining fear, went on. Just outside the walls of Cíbola he was seized. The "sun was about a lance high" when the men of Hawikuh suddenly launched their arrows upon his followers. Some of those who, fleeing, looked back, thought they had seen Estevanico fall beneath that thick hail of darts.

"It is to be believed that a long time ago, when roofs lay over the walls of Kya-ki-me, when smoke hung over the house-tops, and the ladder-rounds were still unbroken in Kya-ki-me, then the Black Mexicans came from their abodes in Everlasting Summerland. . . . Then and thus was killed by our ancients, right where the stone stands down by the arroyo of Kya-ki-me, one of the Black Mexicans, a large man, with chilli lips [lips swollen from chilli peppers]. . . . Then the rest ran away, chased by our grandfathers, and went back toward their country in the Land of Everlasting Summer."

So, in part, runs the Zuñi legend, today, concerning the coming and the death of Estevanico, the Black.[1]

Fray Marcos was not only depressed by the news of Estevanico's capture, but he was in danger. The Indians accompanying him, from various villages along his route, had looked on him as a holy man, invulnerable, under the special protection of the morning and evening star, whose sign he made with his fingers in prayer and erected in wood along his way; for so did they construe the cross, their own symbol for the mystical glory heralding the dawn and the night. Now they were afraid. The friar, after prayer for guidance, opened his bales and, by means of gifts, entreaties, and threats, persuaded them to go on. Even information that surely pointed to Estevanico's death — brought by more Indians, wounded and bleeding — did not deter him. He would at least have a glimpse of that city, if he might not enter it. So from a plateau, looking north, Fray Marcos saw the pueblo of Hawikuh on a bare hill outlined against the high timbered flank of the Zuñi Mountains. Through the rarefied air, to which

[1] Lowery, *Spanish Settlements*, pp. 281–82, as transcribed by Frank Cushing, authority on Zuñi lore and a Zuñi by adoption

the monk's eyes were not accustomed, the pueblo appeared much nearer than it was and therefore much larger. He raised a mound of stones, surmounted by a little cross, "having no implements at hand to make it larger," and took possession of the city he could see — and of all cities beyond which he could not see — and named them the New Kingdom of San Francisco. Then he hastened after his Indians, who had not waited for him, on the homeward trail. "I returned," he says, "with more fear than victuals." In spite of the changed demeanor of the tribe on his way back, he reached New Galicia in safety.

In the City of Mexico the descriptions by Fray Marcos of the great city, as he believed he had seen it with his very eyes, caused a tumult. Another Mexico had at last been found! The discovery was proudly proclaimed from every pulpit. It passed from mouth to mouth among the cavalier adventurers, dicing and dueling away their time and impatient for richer hazards and hotter work for their swords. Such a tale loses nothing by oft telling. It may be that the enthusiasm of his audiences even confused the monk's memory somewhat, as he told the story over and over, even to his barber; for he pictured those distant cities as a paradise on earth, until nothing was now thought of by any man but how to reach Cíbola and be rich forevermore.

In a few weeks Mendoza had enlisted a company of three hundred to serve under Coronado. The majority were of the gentry. Coronado assembled his men at Compostela, near the Pacific coast in New Galicia, in February, 1540; and thither went the Viceroy the long journey from Mexico to send them off with appropriate pomp. It was the most brilliant review yet held in New Spain. Most of the cavaliers were astride of the best horses from the stock farms, and had equipped them with colored blankets trailing almost to the ground, besides leathern armor and silver-mounted harness. Their own mail was polished like woven silver, and the tips of their lances, held erect, flickered in the sun like sparks of fire. Their helmets were of iron or tough bullhide. In their train marched the foot soldiers armed with crossbow and arquebus, some, too, with swords and shield. The third division of the army was composed of several hundred Indian allies, their naked bodies splashed with black, ocher, and vermilion; and their faces, painted terribly for war, surmounted by the green and yellow and crimson plumage of parrots. At royal expense the expedition was equipped with pack-mules, cannon, and a thousand horses. For food on the way and to stock the new country there were droves of cattle and sheep, goats, and swine. Leading all this splendor, and dulling it by his own brighter glory, rode Coronado in golden armor. If the gray robe of Fray Marcos showed but dingily amid this military brilliance, yet it drew the awed glances of the spectators no less than the golden scales of Coronado's coat. This shining army, after all, had still to see what the humble monk in the drab gown had already seen — the magical cities of Cíbola.

To coöperate with Coronado by water, the seaman Alarcón was sent up the coast with three vessels. Alarcón sailed to the head of the Gulf of California and ascended the Colorado River eighty-five leagues, perhaps as far as Yuma. Coronado divided his land forces. Leaving the main body at Culiacán in charge of Arellano, who was later one of the unsuccessful *adelantados* of Florida, Coronado pushed on ahead with Fray Marcos and his brother monks, eighty horse, twenty-five foot soldiers, some Indians and negroes, and part of the artillery. A month later he passed through Vaca's Town of the Hearts; and, continuing north over the divide into the San Pedro valley, he turned eastward and skirted the Santa Catalina mountains to a small Indian settlement in the vicinity of Fort Grant. Here he turned northward again, crossed the Gila, and, after fifteen days of hard march, reached the Zuñi River. Some twenty miles farther on, Coronado and his men caught their first glimpse of Hawikuh. The disappointing sight was like a dash of icewater. Says Castañeda, the historian of the expedition: "When they saw the first village, which was Cíbola, such were the curses that some hurled at Friar Marcos that I pray God may protect him from them. It is a little, crowded village, looking as if it had been crumpled all up together."

The ruins of Hawikuh, fifteen miles southwest of Zuñi, today bear out the description of the disgusted Castañeda. This first of the Seven Cities, however, was not to be taken without a fight. The Zuñi warriors hurled stones on the Spaniards. The golden-plated Coronado was felled and would have been killed but for the heroism of one of his officers who "bestrode him like a good knight, shielded him and dragged him to safety." But the Spaniards could not be resisted. They entered the village and found food there, which was the thing they were most in need of.

Coronado renamed this hill stronghold Granada — possibly in irony — and sojourned there until recovered from his wounds. A deputation of Indians came to him to make peace, while the rest of the tribesmen removed to their war towns on Thunder Mountain. Once more fit for the saddle, Coronado set about the pacification of the province; then sent an expedition to Tusayán, the present Moqui towns in Arizona, and messengers to Mexico with reports to Mendoza. With them went Fray Marcos, "because he did not think it was safe for him to stay in Cíbola, seeing that his report had turned out to be entirely false, because the Kingdoms he had told about had not been found, nor the populous cities, nor the wealth of gold, nor the precious stones which he had reported, nor the fine clothes, nor other things that had been proclaimed from the pulpits." Thus did Castañeda, the historian, twenty years later bitterly enumerate the list of disappointments experienced by himself and others of Coronado's army in the province of the Seven Cities.

While Coronado was at Hawikuh, or "Granada," detachments of his army were penetrating

other sections of the new country. Arellano, with
the main body left at Culiacán, was marching to
Cíbola. Melchior Díaz, one of Coronado's ablest
scouts, was trying to make junction with Alarcón's
ships. Díaz touched the Colorado River some
distance above its mouth. He found letters left
by Alarcón, and met the giant Yuma Indians —
perhaps in the vicinity of the city of Yuma, where
the Gila River empties into the Colorado. These
Indians were then as now of unusual height and
powerfully made, so that one man could lift a log
which several Spaniards could not move. They
went stark naked and in cold weather carried fire-
brands to keep them warm. So Díaz called the
Colorado Río del Tizon, or Firebrand River. Here
Díaz died from an accidental lance thrust, and his
band returned to Sonora.

Meanwhile a report from the Moqui country
came to Coronado of a great river flowing far
down between red mountain walls. This news
inspired Coronado to send López de Cárdenas —
the "good knight" who had saved his life — to
have a look at it; and here is the description of
Grand Canyon by Cárdenas, the first white man
to view the great gorge of the Colorado, as set down
by Castañeda:

After they had gone twenty days' march they came to the banks of a river, which are so high that from the edge of one bank to the other appeared to be three or four leagues in the air. The country was elevated and full of low twisted pines, very cold, and lying open toward the north. . . . They spent three days on this bank looking for a passage down to the river, which looked from above as if the water were six feet across, although the Indians said it was half a league wide. It was impossible to descend, for after these three days Captain Melgosa and one Juan Galeras and another companion, who were the three lightest and most agile men, made an attempt to go down at the least difficult place, and went down until those who were above were unable to keep sight of them. They returned about four o'clock in the afternoon, not having succeeded in reaching the bottom on account of the great difficulties. . . . They said they had been down about a third of the way and that the river seemed very large from the place which they reached. . . . Those who stayed above had estimated that some huge rocks on the sides of the cliffs seemed to be about as tall as a man, but those who went down swore that when they reached these rocks they were bigger than the great tower of Seville.[1]

While Cárdenas was looking at the Grand Canyon, some Indians, led by one whom the Spaniards nicknamed Bigotes (Whiskers), came to Zuñi from the east. They told of great towns, and brought

[1] Winship, *The Coronado Expedition*, p. 489. The Giralda, or famous bell-tower of the Cathedral of Seville, is 275 feet high.

a picture of a buffalo drawn on a piece of hide. Vaca had told of "humpbacked cows," and here were people who lived on the very borders of the cow country. So Hernando de Alvarado was sent east with twenty men, instructed to return within eighty days, and Fray Juan de Padilla went with him. Some fifty miles east of Zuñi Alvarado came on the famous pueblo of Ácoma, or People of the White Rock, three hundred and fifty-seven feet in the air. Ácoma was so lofty, says Casta-ñeda "that it was a very good musket that could throw a ball as high." A broad stairway of about two hundred steps began the ascent, then one hundred narrower steps followed; and "at the top they had to go up about three times as high as a man by means of holes in the rock, in which they put the points of their feet, holding on at the same time by their hands. There was a wall of large and small stones at the top, which they could roll down without showing themselves, so that no army could possibly be strong enough to capture the village. On the top they had room to sow and store a large amount of corn, and cisterns to collect snow and water." The natives came down to the plain and at first offered battle, but presently consented to make peace.

Proceeding eastward, Alvarado went a week's journey beyond to the Tigua villages lying above Albuquerque on both sides of the Río Grande. Pressing on, he visited the towns of Cicuyé, or Pecos (in the valley of the upper Pecos River and at the foot of the Santa Fé mountains) and the Buffalo Plains to the east. The Pecos Indians received him warmly and escorted him into the town "with drums and pipes something like flutes" and gave him presents of cloth and turquoises.

By the close of autumn Coronado's several detachments reassembled in the village of Tiguex near the site of Bernalillo, above Albuquerque. Here they listened to tales of a new El Dorado from an Indian whom Alvarado had picked up and had dubbed El Turco (the Turk) "because he looked like one." The new El Dorado was called Quivira. El Turco said that in Quivira, which was his own country and far to the east, there was a river two leagues wide, where fish as big as horses sported themselves. Great numbers of huge canoes, with twenty rowers on a side and with high carved golden prows thrusting up among their white sails, floated on its surface like water lilies on a pond. The chief of that country took his afternoon nap under a tall spreading tree decorated

with an infinitude of little golden bells on which
gentle zephyrs played his lullaby.   Even the com-
mon folk there had their ordinary dishes made of
"wrought plate"; and the pitchers and bowls were
of solid gold.   El Turco could readily prove his
tale if only he could recover his wonderful golden
bracelets of which he had been robbed by the
natives of Cicuyé, the town of Chief Whiskers'
countrymen where Alvarado had recently been
entertained with such hospitality and good will.

So Coronado sent Alvarado back to Cicuyé to
demand the bracelets.   The natives of Cicuyé
bluntly said that El Turco was a liar; whereupon
Alvarado put Whiskers and the head chief, a very
old man, in chains.   Enraged at this treachery,
the Indians took up their arrows and drove the
Spaniards out, denouncing them as men who had
no respect for their word.   "This began the want
of confidence in the word of the Spaniards when-
ever there was talk of peace from this time on,"
says Castañeda.   Coronado followed up the seizure of Whiskers and the old chief of Cicuyé by a
levy of three hundred *mantas*, or pieces of cloth.
The Tiguas, not having the *mantas*, were stripped
of their garments.   A Spanish officer forcibly possessed himself of an Indian's handsome young wife.

The Indians rose. In the mêlée the Spaniards were victorious; and presently the natives, from the roofs, were making their symbol of peace — the cross sign of the evening and morning star. The Spaniards made the same sign by crossing their spears. The natives threw down their arms. Contrary to the peace pledge, some two hundred of them were seized and stakes were erected to burn them. Seeing the rest of their number "beginning to roast," a hundred captives made valiant, if futile, efforts to defend themselves. Only one or two escaped to warn their friends that Spaniards speaking peace must never again be trusted.

Heavy snows and severe cold so hampered the army during the winter that not until early in spring was the surrounding country "pacified." A great many Indians had been slain, but many more had escaped to their mountain retreats. In vain had Coronado sent deputations seeking peace. The invariable answer was that the Spaniards were false men who had desecrated the star symbol, the sign of inviolable peace; the wind of the desert might hearken to their promises, but never the Indians. So when Coronado took up his march he left implacable enemies in his wake.

But the "great good news of the Turk gave no little joy," and the restless conqueror prepared to set out for Golden Quivira.   Among the Indians news traveled fast, and it is easy to imagine the consternation felt by the tribes of the lower Mississippi Valley, in the spring of 1541, to hear of the approach of the two great invading expeditions from opposite directions, each of which was conquering every tribe and village on the way.   De Soto had reached Tampa Bay in 1539, just about the time when Fray Marcos came in view of Cíbola.   Coronado had left Culiacán when De Soto was on the Savannah River; when Coronado reached the Río Grande pueblos, De Soto was marching south through Alabama toward Mobile Bay.   While Coronado was in winter quarters at Tiguex, on the Río Grande, in New Mexico, De Soto was in camp at the Chickasaw town in Mississippi; and now Coronado entered the Texas plains shortly before De Soto crossed the Mississippi.

On April 23, 1541, Coronado set out under the guidance of El Turco; and four days later crossed the Pecos in the vicinity of Puerto de Luna, New Mexico.   He continued in an easterly course across the great plains (where the Arab-like

Apaches roved and hailed him fearlessly from the doors of their painted skin tents) and into Texas. Here enormous herds of buffalo provided an abundance of meat. Castañeda speaks of seeing the skyline between the legs of bison grazing at a distance. "This country," he says, "is like a bowl, so that when a man sits down, the horizon surrounds him all around at the distance of a musket shot." The plains baffled the hunting parties. They wandered in circles about the heaps of "cows" they had killed until musket shots from the main camp gave them direction; and some hunters were lost. It seemed as if the vast prairie itself designed the destruction of the strangers who had invaded its solitude, for it wiped out their trails as the sea obliterates the mark of the keel. Castañeda exclaims, wonderingly: "Who could believe that a thousand horses and five hundred of our cows, and more than five thousand rams and ewes, and more than fifteen hundred friendly Indians and servants. in travelling over these plains, would leave no more trace where they had passed than if nothing had been there — nothing — so that it was necessary to make piles of bones and cow-dung now and then so that the rear-guard could follow the army. The grass never failed to become erect after it had been trodden down, and although it was short, it was as fresh and straight as before."

June found the army among the Teyas Indians in western Texas. By this time so many of El Turco's tales had been disproved that he traveled in irons. Food and water became scarce. Most important of all, the Teyas guides told Coronado that Quivira was north, not east. Coronado therefore ordered the main body, under Arellano, back to Tiguex, in New Mexico. He himself, with only thirty horsemen and six footmen, would push north, to follow the new directions. In vain his men besought him not to leave them leaderless. The melancholy induced, even in seasoned plainsmen at times, by the broad monotonous stretches of prairie obsessed them. They feared that death would halt them somewhere on their lost march and toss their skeletons among the buffalo bones sprinkling that relentless land which had refused their impress as conquerors. They feared to see their general's gleaming casque disappear once and forever over the northern rim of the sky, leaving no more trace than the wing of a golden eagle passing through the ether. But Coronado stubbornly held on his way —

"Still nursing the unconquerable hope,
Still clutching the inviolable shade."

The army separated near the upper waters of
the Brazos.   After some thirty days Coronado and
his little band crossed the Arkansas into Kansas.
They continued in a northeasterly direction and,
about a week later, reached the first of the Quivira
towns in the vicinity of Great Bend, Kansas,
where, then and for centuries after, lived Wichita Indians.   Here no sparkling sails floated like
petals on the clear surface of an immeasurable
stream.   No lordly chief drowsed to the murmur
of innumerable bells.   The water pitchers on the
shoulders of the women, stooping in the low en-
trances of their grass-thatched huts, were not
golden.   "Neither gold nor silver nor any trace of
either was found among these people."   El Turco
confessed that he had been detailed by the tribesmen of those whom Coronado had incinerated to
lead the lying strangers out on the plains "and
lose them."   Wandering over the sun-baked prairie, food and water failing and their horses dying, the Spaniards would become so weak that
should any return, the Tiguas could "kill them
without any trouble, and thus they could take revenge for what had been done to them . . . as

for gold he did not know where there was any of it."

So Coronado had the Turk garroted, and set up a cross with the inscription, "Francisco Vasquez de Coronado, general of an expedition, reached this place." Then he turned back, empty-handed; for even explorers whom he had sent out northward, and who may have reached the Nebraska line, had found no sign of rich peoples nor of precious metals. Meanwhile Arellano had reached Tiguex safely. Arrived there some weeks later, Coronado sent out exploring parties, one of which visited Taos, that interesting town still lying between the Río Hondo and the Taos Mountains. Here the Spaniards found a high type of Indian civilization, large well-stocked granaries, and wooden bridges flung across the Taos River to connect the eighteen divisions of the town.[1]

Winter bore hard on Coronado's men, who were on scant rations and almost naked. The officers seized the most and the best of everything for themselves, and dangerous dissensions arose in

[1] Taos today has about 425 Indian inhabitants; and it is also the home of a small but noted school of American painters, who are bringing the life and character of the Pueblo Indians and the color and atmosphere of the southwestern mesas prominently into American art.

the camp. Towards the end of winter Coronado, riding at the ring on a festival day, fell beneath the hoofs of his companion's horse and was dangerously injured in the head. His illness and his failures preyed on his mind; and he resolved to seek no farther for wealth, but to return to his wife in Mexico. In April, 1542, he and his disappointed band turned homeward. At that very time, far to the east, Hernando de Soto also was giving up the Golden Quest and turning his face towards Mexico, to die of a broken spirit a month later. Hungry and tattered, and harassed by Indians, Coronado and his army painfully made their way back towards New Galicia. The soldiers were in open revolt; they dropped out by the score and went on pillaging forays at their pleasure. With barely a hundred followers, Coronado presented himself before Mendoza, bringing with him nothing more precious than the gold-plated armor in which he had set out two years before. He had enriched neither himself nor his King, so his end is soon told: "he lost his reputation, and shortly thereafter the government of New Galicia."

Two soldiers had been left in Kansas; their fate is not known. Fray Juan Padilla, Fray Juan de la Cruz, and a lay brother, Luís Descalona,

remained with six companions in New Mexico
The friars were resolved to bring about the conversion of these Indians, whose settled modes of
living seemed to promise a good opportunity. La
Cruz, an old man, was well treated at first by the
chiefs at Tiguex but was killed eventually. Descalona went east to the Pecos River and presumably was slain. Fray Juan Padilla, with a
Portuguese, two oblates, and some native guides
went back to Quivira, that is, to Kansas. He
won the love of the Indians of that region; but, not
content with this harvest, he set out for the towns
of some of their foes. On the way he was murdered, either by natives of the towns he sought or
by his own guides from Tiguex. The Portuguese
and the two oblates witnessed his martyrdom from
a neighboring hill; and in time they made their
way across Oklahoma and Texas to Pánuco, where
they told the story. And, says a Spanish writer of
the day, it was then recalled that "great prodigies"
were seen at his death, "as it were the earth
flooded, globes of fire, comets, and obscurations of
the sun."

Today we may doubt the pious historian's
"great prodigies." But we look over that land,
where many temple spires rise in security to

proclaim one Christ, however variously sought,
and we are moved to honor the zeal and devotion
of Fray Juan Padilla and his two brother monks
— the first unarmed mission of the Church upon
the soil of the United States.

"Know that on the right hand of the Indies
there is an island called California, very close to
the side of the Terrestrial Paradise; and it was
peopled by black women, without any man among
them, for they lived in the fashion of Amazons.
They were of strong and hardy bodies, of ardent
courage and great force. Their island was the
strongest in all the world, with its steep cliffs and
rocky shores. Their arms were all of gold, and
so was the harness of the wild beasts which they
tamed to ride; for in the whole island there was no
metal but gold." So wrote Montalvo, the author
of *Esplandián*, a romance which, first published in
1510, rapidly became the "best seller" of its day,
running through at least four editions. This book
may have influenced the Emperor Charles V in
banning fiction from the Indies, where the imaginations of both Spaniards and natives needed no
artificial stimulation. At all events, both Spaniards and Indians were forbidden to peruse these

romances.　Probably the Indians obeyed the wise decree.　But evidently in the case of the Spaniards the mischief had already been done; and hence the name, California, applied long since to a region which has seen more romance and produced more gold than ever were conceived of in the imagination of the ancient Spanish author.

The legend of the Amazons was curiously interwoven with both the discovery and the naming of California.　While Guzmán and Coronado were moving north by land others were advancing by sea.　Cortés, conqueror of Mexico, was urged north especially by rumors of a rich province inhabited only by women, like the island in Montalvo's tale.　His nephew, Francisco Cortés, was sent from Colima to follow the clue (1524).　The Amazon province was not found, nor yet was belief in it shattered.　Nine years later Jiménez, one of Cortés's explorers, discovered the Peninsula of Lower California, thought it to be an island, and reported it to have pearls.　A pearl bearing island, "down the coast toward India," fitted in with Cortés's notions of geography.　So he personally led a colony to the "island," which he named Santa Cruz.

The dismal failure of the colony was only a

temporary discouragement. Hoping to forestall Viceroy Mendoza, Cortés rushed an exploring expedition north under Francisco de Ulloa (1539). Nearly a year before Alarcón, whom Mendoza sent to aid Coronado, Ulloa reached the head of the Gulf, rounded the peninsula, and returned with the news that it was not after all an island, but *tierra firme*. Now the name Santa Cruz gave way to "California," the change being a new application of the old belief in the Amazon island, as recorded in Montalvo's novel. Perhaps Cortés, grim soldier, had a passion for light reading — even as today captains of industry refresh themselves with Sherlock Holmes — for the historian Herrera states that it was he who bestowed the name upon the peninsula which he tried in vain to colonize. Possibly the name was bestowed in derision, but just when, or how, or by whom, no one has established with certainty.

Ulloa's voyage marks the close of Cortés's efforts to explore the northern Pacific, but the work was continued by Viceroy Mendoza. Through the death of Alvarado, the dashing conqueror of Guatemala, in the Mixton War (1541), Mendoza inherited a fleet which had been prepared for exploration in the Pacific, and with it he carried out Alvarado's plans by dispatching two expeditions, one up the California coast, the other across the Pacific.

The expedition "in the West towards China or the Spice Islands" was led by López de Villalobos. Sailing in November, 1542, he took possession of the Philippine Islands and thus attached them to Mexico. Villalobos died in the Moluccas; his enterprise went to pieces; but the voyage made a link between California and the Philippines.

Mendoza's other sea expedition, which was to explore along the outer coast of the peninsula and northward in search of the Strait of Anian and new provinces, left Mexico on June 27, 1542, under command of Juan Rodríguez Cabrillo. At this date Hernando de Soto's body had been consigned to the Father of Waters and his defeated army led by Moscoso was marching west across Arkansas in search of Pánuco, and Coronado with a hundred ragged followers was returning to Compostella after two fruitless years in New Mexico and the Buffalo Plains.

Of Cabrillo little is known except that he was a Portuguese by birth and a skilled mariner; and he is supposed to have been in the service of Cortés during the conquest of Mexico. With two vessels

smaller than any coasting schooner of today, badly
built and scantily outfitted — a crew chiefly composed of conscripts and natives, and the sturdy
Levantine pilot, Bartolomé Ferrelo, or Ferrer,
Cabrillo departed on the trail of adventure.   Owing to calms and contrary winds and the frequent
necessity to heave to and send ashore for fresh
water, his progress was slow.   By the 10th of
August he had passed the most northerly point
reached by Ulloa.   Eleven days later he landed at
the bay of San Quentín and took possession in the
name of the King.   Here a week was spent in
taking in water and repairing sails and in receiving
friendly visits from Indians who said that they had
seen other Spaniards in the interior — probably
some of Alarcón's or Coronado's band.   The diarist of the expedition says that these Indians were
smeared with a "white paste" in such a fashion
that "they appeared like men in hose and slashed
doublets."   On the 28th of September, Cabrillo
discovered "a port closed and very good, which
they named San Miguel."   This was the beautiful
Bay of San Diego.   On the purpled blue waters of
this bay, safely sheltered by the long high stretch
of Point Loma, their ships rode at anchor while a
terrific storm raged without for three days.

When the gale had subsided Cabrillo continued northward. He discovered the islands of Santa Catalina and San Clemente, and the pleasant Bay of Santa Monica, which he called the Bay of the Smokes, or Bay of the Fires, because of the low curling clouds of blue smoke rising from the Indian villages along its shores. On the 10th of October he went ashore at San Buenaventura, where he visited an Indian settlement which he called the Town of Canoes, in allusion to the excellent craft which the natives possessed. Then, sailing west, he passed through the Santa Bárbara Channel and on the eighteenth reached Point Conception, which he named Cabo de Galera because it was shaped like a galley. Here northwest winds drove him into Cuyler's harbor on San Miguel Island.

Two weeks later a southwester filled Cabrillo's sails and carried his vessels round the cape and along the high rocky coast, where the Santa Lucía Mountain comes down to the sea. Below Point Pinos the vessels were driven northward by a storm and became separated. Having missed the Bay of Monterey, Half Moon Bay, and the Golden Gate, Cabrillo turned back and discovered the harbor where Drake cast anchor twenty-five years later, and which is still known as Drake's Bay. Apparently Cabrillo now stood well out to sea, for again he missed the Golden Gate and Monterey Bay.

He put into San Miguel Island for winter; and there "on the 3d of the month of January, 1543, Juan Rodríguez Cabrillo, captain of the said ships, departed from this life, as the result of a fall which he suffered on said island when they were there before, from which he broke an arm near the shoulder . . . at the time of his death he emphatically charged them not to leave off exploring as much as possible all that coast." So, in a few words, we are told all we know of the character of Cabrillo, who had battered his way up the California coast in the pain of an injury sufficient to bring him to death, and whose last words to his men were to press on. His bones lie under the white sands of San Miguel Island, undiscovered yet — save perhaps by some Portuguese or Levantine fisherman of a later time, driving the supports of his driftwood shack deep down through the shifting sand.

The command now devolved upon the pilot Ferrelo. Though frequently halted and swept about by heavy storms and suffering from diminished supplies, this fearless mariner, obeying his

master's behest, held on northward. He sailed
to a point near the mouth of Rogue River, Oregon,
when he turned back, through "travail" worse
than any Cabrillo had experienced. On April 14,
1543, he reached the home port of Navidad.

Interest in California was revived by developments in the Far East. Though Villalobos had
taken possession of the Philippines in the year of
Ferrelo's voyage, the Spaniards had not occupied
the islands. But in 1559 Philip II, tempted by the
profits accruing to the Portuguese from their spice
trade, ordered Velasco, the Mexican Viceroy, to
equip an expedition for discovery among those
islands and to search out a route for return voyages
to Mexico — for the problem of the return voyage had hitherto baffled mariners. In 1564, after
many delays, Miguel López de Legazpi set sail
from Navidad and, in the following year, took
possession of the Philippines. Legazpi sent one
of his vessels, with his chief navigator, Fray Andrés de Urdaneta, to discover the return route to
New Spain. Urdaneta, turning northward, entered
the Japan current, which carried him to the coast
of northern California whence he descended to
Mexico. By a happy combination of chance and

science he had solved the problem of the return route. Thus a regular trade route was established from Manila to Mexico and thence to Spain. The Manila galleons sailed the course marked out by Urdaneta, across the Pacific to a point off Cape Mendocino and down the coast to Acapulco. It was a hard voyage and frequently the vessels reached the American coast much in need of repairs and with a loss of half the crew from scurvy. There was therefore need of a port on the northern coast. Also, Spanish interests in the Pacific were threatened by the possibility that English, French, or Dutch freebooters in the Atlantic might discover the Strait of Anian and take control of the direct route to the Spice Islands even as Portugal rad formerly monopolized the African route. In fact, Drake, who appeared on the California coast in 1579, having plundered Spanish harbors and a Manila galleon on his northward trip, was believed to have discovered the Strait and to have sailed homeward through it. Six years later, Cavendish looted and burned the *Santa Ana*, a Manila galleon, off California. Dutch mariners rounded Cape Horn, whose name commemorates one of them, and pushed their operations into the western seas. And Spain's Armada had been destroyed by Drake, the

8

man who, it was feared, knew the whereabouts of the Strait of Anian.

To meet the emergency, Cermeño, commander of one of the Philippine galleons, was sent on his return from Manila to seek a port on the California coast, but he was wrecked in Drake's Bay (1595). His cargo of beeswax and fine porcelain still lies at the bottom of the bay, awaiting a modern treasure seeker.

At the same time Sebastian Vizcaíno was commissioned to colonize Lower California as a defensive outpost. Vizcaíno was a prosperous merchant in the Manila trade. He had been aboard the *Santa Ana* when Cavendish attacked her. Because he did not belong to the aristocratic class from which Spain selected her conquerors, even Velasco was opposed to him and chose him chiefly for want of any one else suitable for the work. Vizcaíno planted a colony at La Paz in 1597, but the Indians broke it up. He returned, defeated but not disheartened, and secured a new contract, after several years of delay, having at last won over the new Viceroy, the Count of Monterey, who was forced to admit that Vizcaíno possessed more ability than he had expected to find in a mere merchant. When Vizcaíno had finally made his

way through the maze of red tape to the command
of three vessels and a company of soldiers, the
Spanish monopoly in the Far East had received
a shock; for the British East India Company,
formed in 1600, had carried the trade war into
the Orient, where — by reason of the recent union
with Portugal — Spain had thought herself secure.
Thus did the importance of the direct route to the
East magnify from year to year.

On May 5, 1602, Vizcaíno sailed from Acapulco.
He made detailed explorations along the outer
coast and among the islands and was retarded
frequently by high winds, so that it was November
when he dropped anchor in San Miguel Bay, to
which he gave its present name of San Diego.

On the 16th of December occurred the capital
event of the voyage, the discovery of Monterey
Bay. At seven in the evening Vizcaíno entered
the harbor. On the next day he sent an officer
ashore "to make a hut where Mass could be said
and to see if there was water, and what the country
was like. He found that there was fresh water
and a great oak near the shore, where he made the
hut and arbor to say Mass," writes Father Ascensión, who accompanied the expedition. Because
of the shortage of men and supplies, Vizcaíno

decided to send a ship back to Mexico from this port asking for more men and provisions.

Vizcaíno proceeded northwards, making careful examination of the coast, yet missing that treasure of waters lying behind the great pillars of Golden Gate, and came to anchor in Drake's Bay, from which he was driven almost immediately by off-shore winds. On January 12, 1603, he reached Cape Mendocino, which his orders cited, in very general terms, as the northern limit of his explorations. Off the Cape he encountered so furious a wind, "together with so much rain and fog, as to throw us into great doubt whether to go forward or to turn back, for it was as dark in the daytime as at night." A council was held to decide whether to continue or to return; and the condition of the crew seemed to make retreat imperative. For a week, however, storms from the south prevented the return; and on the seventeenth, at night, Vizcaíno's ship was struck "by two seas which made it pitch so much that it was thought the keel was standing on end, and that it was even sinking." The violent motion threw "both sick and well from their beds." Vizcaíno was flung with such force upon some boxes that he "broke his ribs with the heavy blow." The diarist concludes that "the currents and seas" were carrying them "rapidly to the Strait of Anian," for they were in forty-two degrees of latitude, when a light northwest wind enabled them to head southward and "brought us out of this trouble."

Though the friendly Indians of Monterey signaled to them with smoke as they passed, they did not enter the harbor because the state of health aboard was so bad, "and the sick were clamoring, although there was neither assistance nor medicines, nor food to give them except rotten jerked beef, gruel, biscuits, and beans and chick-peas spoiled by weevils."

Vizcaíno and his crew arrived at Mazatlan in February, 1603, "in the greatest affliction and travail ever experienced by Spaniards; for the sick were crying aloud, while those who were able to walk or to go on all fours were unable to manage the sails." Here Vizcaíno himself, regardless of his feeble condition, set off inland on foot to bring relief from the nearest town to his companions. In a month they were able to set sail for Acapulco where they arrived on the 21st of March, and learned that most of the men on the ship which Vizcaíno had sent back from Monterey for more men and supplies, had died on the way. Later, on reaching the City of Mexico, they found the crew of the third ship, a frigate, which they had believed lost in the hurricane off Mendocino. It seems that the frigate had sailed one degree farther north, to a point named in the diary Cape Blanco: and her crew told of a large river which they had seen.

By placing that "river" several degrees too far north, the mapmakers and historians of that day set going another myth which was to rival the Strait of Anian — the myth of the River of the West. And as the fable of the Strait was to lead to the discovery of Bering Strait, so the myth of the River of the West was to end with the later discovery of the Columbia.

The Count of Monterey immediately planned to occupy the port bearing his name and naturally selected Vizcaíno to lead the enterprise. But, during the inevitable delays between plan and action, a new viceroy succeeded Monterey, and the plan was abandoned for a project to found a port in the mid-Pacific. With this in view, in 1611 Vizcaíno was sent out to explore some islands called suggestively Rica de Oro and Rica de Plata — Rich in Gold and Rich in Silver. Nothing came of this venture; and so Vizcaíno, ruined in health and fortune, fades out of the pages of historical narrative, though he is known to have lived for some years afterwards. And the history of Alta California remained obscure in the fog for a hundred and sixty years.

CHAPTER V

FLORIDA

EXPLORERS first, then colonizers. Now interest in Florida, already aroused by the journey of Vaca, was quickened to a lively heat when, late in 1543, Moscoso and the remnants of De Soto's band at last straggled into the City of Mexico. It would appear that hardships and failures could in no wise impair a Spaniard's ability for story-telling; for Moscoso and his tattered comrades were soon spinning for others the golden web of romance in which they themselves had been snared. Glowing pictures they gave of the north country, especially of Coosa (in Alabama), where they had been well fed and where one or two of their number had remained to dally with Creek damsels. The Viceroy Mendoza, ambitious to extend his power into the Northern Mystery, at once offered to finance an expedition if Moscoso would undertake it. But while Moscoso's zeal for golden Florida might inspire his imagination to dazzling flights of fancy, it was inadequate to stir his feet one step again in that direction. So Mendoza's project came to nothing.

It was noticed that the Mexicans valued highly some of the fur apparel brought back by Moscoso's men. And the next year, 1544, two Spanish gentlemen sought from the King the right to conquer Florida, for the purpose of bringing deerskins and furs into Mexico, as well as in the hope of discovering pearls, mines, and whatever other marvels had embroidered Moscoso's romance. But the King refused their petition. In his refusal he was influenced in part by religious and humane motives. Despite the presence of priests and friars, the various expeditions to the north thus far had taken no time from treasure hunting to convert natives or to establish missions. The Church was now considering the question of sending out its own expedition to Florida, unhampered by slave-catching soldiers.

Perhaps this idea of a conquest by the Cross, unaided — and unhampered — by the sword, was born in the mind of Fray Luís Cancer, a devout and learned Dominican. Fray Luís was living in the convent of Santo Domingo in the City of Mexico not long after Vaca and Moscoso arrived

with their wonder tales.   The account of the hundreds of savages who had followed Vaca from village
to village must have moved the good friar's heart
with zeal and pity.   And he can have been no less
stirred by the tales told by Moscoso's men of the
gallant butchery their swords had done — of the
clanking chains that made music on the day's
march, and the sharp whisper in the night of the
flint, as it pressed against an iron collar.   Fray
Luís desired to see all heathen made free in God's
favor.   The oppressions his countrymen practiced
upon the natives filled him with horror.   As a
missionary, first in Española and then in Porto
Rico, he had seen the hopelessness of trying to
spread religion in territories which were being
swiftly depopulated by ruthless conquerors.   He
had therefore gone to Guatemala, to the monastery of Santiago whose head was the noble Las
Casas.   At that time one province of Guatemala
was known as the "Land of War" because of the
ferocity of its natives.   Las Casas had influenced
the Governor to forbid that territory to Spaniards
for five years.   Then he had sent Fray Luís, who
had meanwhile learned the language of the natives,
to the chief to request permission for the monks to
come there.   With his gentle words, Fray Luís

'took also little gifts, trinkets, mirrors, and beads of bright colors such as would delight the savages. He made so good an impression on the chief that the permission he sought was readily given. And in a few years the Land of War became the Land of the True Peace — Vera Paz — where no Spaniards dwelt save a few Dominican friars and where at morning and evening Indian voices chanted the sacred songs to the accompaniment of the Indian flutes and drums which had formerly quickened to frenzy the warriors setting out to slaughter. And for this spiritual conquest Fray Luís had received the title of Alférez de la Fé, Standard Bearer of the Faith.

But Fray Luís was not content to eat the fruit of his labors in Vera Paz. The Standard Bearer would push on to another frontier. He went to the City of Mexico (1546) because there he would find the latest reports of newly discovered countries. Here Fray Luís heard the stories which had been told there by Vaca and Moscoso and resolved to bear his standard to Florida.

He found willing comrades in three monks of his own order, Gregorio de Beteta, Juan García, and Diego de Tolosa. Fray Gregorio and Fray Juan had already made three or four unsuccessful attempts to reach Florida by land from Mexico, under a total misapprehension as to distance and direction. His plans consummated under the orders of Las Casas, Fray Luís went to Spain to urge the great project with the King. His petition was soon granted. When he returned to Mexico (1548) he had the royal authority to establish a mission at some point in Florida where Spaniards had not yet spilled native blood. In 1549 Fray Luís and his three companions sailed from Vera Cruz in an unarmed vessel. At Havana he took on board a converted native girl named Magdalena, who was to act as interpreter and guide. Perhaps it was almost impossible for the pilot to distinguish one inlet from another, with certainty, on that much indented coast line, where the low shore presents no variation to the eye for miles; for, instead of landing at a new point, the monks first touched Florida soil in the vicinity of Tampa Bay. And the natives about Tampa Bay were hostile with memories of De Soto.

There were empty huts nearby and a background of forest in which it seemed nothing stirred Fray Diego went ashore and climbed a tree at some distance from the beach. Immediately a score of Indians emerged from the forest. Fray

Luís, despite the pilot's warnings, with Magdalena and an oblate named Fuentes, hurried after Diego, through water to their waists. "Our Lord knows what haste I made lest they should slay the monk before hearing what we were about," Fray Luís writes. He paused to fall on his knees and pray for grace and divine help, ere he climbed the bank. Then he took out of his sleeves some of the trinkets he had brought; because, he writes, "deeds are love, and gifts shatter rocks."[1] After these gifts, the natives were willing that the friars and Magdalena should kneel among them reciting the litanies; and, to Fray Luís's joy, they also knelt and appeared pleased with the prayers and the rosaries. They seemed so friendly, indeed, that Fray Luís permitted Fray Diego, Fuentes, and Magdalena to remain with them and to go on a day and a half's journey by land to a good harbor of which the Indians had told them. He and Fray Gregorio returned to the ship.

It took the pilot eight days to find the new harbor and eight more to enter it. It was on the feast of Corpus Christi that the ship dropped anchor. Fray Luís and Fray Juan landed and said Mass. To their apprehension they saw no signs of Fray

[1] Lowery, *Spanish Settlements*, p. 420.

Diego and Fuentes, nor of Indians. On the next day as they searched, an Indian came out of the woods carrying, in token of peace, a rod topped with white palm leaves; and he appeared to assure Fray Luís that Fray Diego and his companions were safe and would be brought to him. On the next day as Fray Luís, with Fray Juan and Fray Gregorio, rowed towards the shore the natives waded to meet them bringing fish and skins to trade for trinkets. One savage would take nothing but a little wooden cross which he kissed as he had seen the monks do — much to the delight of Fray Luís. If the pious monk's joy at this incident was dimmed a few moments later, when he waded inshore and discovered Magdalena naked among the tribeswomen, it kindled again at her assurance that Diego and Fuentes were safe in the cacique's house. How little truth was in her words Fray Luís learned when he returned to the ship. There he found a Spaniard, once a soldier of De Soto's army, who had been enslaved by the Indians of this tribe. This man informed him that the Indians had already slain Fray Diego and the oblate Fuentes; he had held Diego's scalp in his hands.

To pleas that he forsake his mission and sail away to safer shores, Fray Luís had but one answer.

Where his comrades in the faith, acting under his orders, had fallen, there would he remain. Though storms prevented him from landing for two days, he refused to accept the assertions of his shipmates — that the storms were sent by God to keep him from a death among savages. And, at last, through the lashing and roaring of sea and wind, he came again to shore. Armed natives painted for war could be seen grouped on the bank above the slope to the beach. "For the love of God wait a little; do not land," Fray Gregorio entreated. But Fray Luís had already leaped into the water. He turned back once, on reaching the beach, but it was to call to Gregorio or Juan to bring to him a small cross he had forgotten. When Gregorio cried, "Father, for mercy's sake, will not your reverence come for it, as there is no one here who will take it to you," Fray Luís went on towards the hill.[1] At its foot he knelt in prayer for a few moments, then began the ascent. Midway the Indians closed about him, swinging their clubs. He cried out once, loudly, before their blows struck him down. Those in the boat heard his cry, and saw the savages clubbing and slashing at his body as they thrust it down the hill. Then a shower of

---

[1] Lowery, *Spanish Settlements*, p. 425.

arrows falling upon their boat made them pull away in haste to the ship. The next day the vessel set sail and, three weeks later, anchored off Vera Cruz.

Philip II had come to the throne the master of Europe. His father, Charles V, had been not only sovereign ruler of Spain, of the Netherlands, of Naples, of a part of central Italy, of Navarre, and Emperor of Germany by election, but he had hoped to become master of England also and to leave in his heir's hands a world all Spanish and all Catholic. Philip II inherited his father's power and his father's dream. If his natural abilities were less, his obstinacy and his zeal were greater. He had seen the march of Spanish power not unattended by affronting incidents. In 1520 a monk named Luther had defied Philip's father, the Emperor, to his face. The Reformation was spreading. Huguenots were powerful in the domestic politics of France; and France was threatening Spain's American possessions. Her fishermen had passed yearly in increasing numbers between the Banks of Newfoundland and their home ports. And a mariner of several cross-sea voyages, one Jacques Cartier, had discovered the St. Lawrence River and had set off again in 1540 to people "a country called Canada."

But these voyages of discovery were not the worst of France's insults to Spain. French pirates had formed the habit of darting down on Spanish treasure ships and appropriating their contents. They had also sacked Spanish ports in the islands. Many of these pirates were Huguenots, "Lutheran heretics," as the Spaniards called them. Another danger also was beginning to appear on the horizon, though it was as yet but a speck. It hailed from England, whose mariners were beginning to fare forth into all seas for trade and plunder. They were trending towards the opinion of King Francis of France, that God had not created the gold of the New World only for Castilians. A train of Spanish treasure displayed in London had set more than one stout seaman to head-scratching over the inequalities of this world and how best to readjust the balances. There was reason enough, then, for Philip's fear that large portions of the New World might readily be snatched from Spain by heretical seamen; and Philip was as fierce in the pursuit of his own power as in his zeal for his religion.

The slow-moving treasure fleets from Mexico

o

and Havana sailed past Florida through the Bahama Channel, which Ponce de León had discovered, and on to the Azores and Spain. The channel was not only the favorite hunting place of pirates — so that the Spanish treasure ships no longer dared go singly but now combined for protection; it was also the home of storms. The fury of its winds had already driven too many vessels laden with gold upon the Florida coast, where as yet there were no ports of succor. Cargoes had thus been wholly lost, and sailors and passengers murdered by the savages. To these dangers was added the fear that the French designed to plant a colony on the Florida coast near the channel, so that they might seize Spanish vessels in case of war, for not one could pass without their seeing it.

So, on Philip's order, Viceroy Velasco bestirred himself to raise a colony, not only for Coosa but for some other point in Florida. The other point selected was Santa Elena, now Port Royal, South Carolina. When all was ready, the company comprised no less than fifteen hundred persons. Of the twelve captains in the force, six had been with De Soto. In the party there were Coosa women who had followed the Spaniards to Mexico. They were now homeward bound. At the head of the colony went Tristán de Luna y Arellano, the same Don Tristán who had been Coronado's second in command in the Cíbola enterprise eighteen years before. The departure of the expedition was celebrated with great pomp. Velasco himself crossed the mountains to Vera Cruz to see it off.

But this expedition was to be another record of disaster and failure. Arellano brought his fleet to anchor in Pensacola Bay; and thence dispatched three vessels for Santa Elena. Before his supplies were unloaded, a tremendous hurricane swept the Bay and destroyed most of his ships with great loss of life. So violent was the storm that it tossed one vessel, like a nutshell, upon the green shore. Some of the terror-struck soldiers saw the shrieking demons of Hell striding the low, racing, black clouds. The outguards of the storm attacked the three ships bound for the Carolina coast and drove them south, so that they returned to Mexico by way of Cuba.

The survivors at Pensacola Bay were soon in straits for food. So Arellano, leaving a garrison on the coast, sent about a thousand of his colonists — men, women, and children — to Santa Cruz de Nanipacna, forty leagues inland on a large river, probably in Monroe County, Alabama. But these colonists in the fruitful land were like the seventeen-year locusts; they ate everything from the Indians' stores of maize and beans to palm-shoots, acorns, and grass seeds — but produced nothing. And soon an exploring band of three hundred was sent on towards famed Coosa in search of more food. They reached it after a hundred days of weary marching over De Soto's old trail. Though the natives had small reason to love De Soto's countrymen, they treated the Spaniards well and fed them bountifully all summer. Twelve men, sent back to Nanipacna with reports, reached that place at last, to find only a deserted camp and a letter saying that the famished colony had returned to Pensacola. When Arellano wished to go to Coosa to see for himself if it were suitable for a colony, his people mutinied. The malcontents sent a spurious order to the explorers at Coosa to return; and in November, 1560, after more than a year in the interior, the little band joined the main body at Pensacola.

Two ships, which Arellano had sent home for aid, reached Mexico safely. The Viceroy immediately sent provisions for the colonists and a new leader, Angel de Villafañe, to replace Arellano and to enjoy those high-sounding but, so far, empty titles bestowed upon the successive Governors of Florida. Villafañe's orders were to move the colonists to Santa Elena. Pensacola was too far westward for Philip's chief purpose; the most important matter was to establish a colony on the Atlantic seaboard where it could keep a watchful eye on the French, should they venture too far south of Cartier's river. Fray Gregorio de Beteta, who had been with Fray Luís Cancer of martyr fame, accompanied Villafañe in the hope that the natives of Carolina would prove less recalcitrant than those about Tampa Bay. Villafañe provisioned the garrison at Pensacola and then set sail for Santa Elena. At Havana many of his followers deserted him; but, in May, with the residue, he reached the Carolina coast. He explored as far as Cape Hatteras, but found no site which he considered suitable for colonization. So he abandoned the project and returned to Española in July, 1561. A ship was soon dispatched to remove the garrison left at Pensacola.

The failure of the Spaniards thus far to effect a settlement on the coast of the Atlantic mainland of North America is readily explicable. In the islands, in Mexico, and South America, the Spaniards

flourished because of the precious metals and the
docility of the natives. On the northern mainland they found no mines, and the Indians would
not submit to enslavement. They traversed a rich
game country and great tracts of fertile soil
which, later, the English settler's rifle and plow
were to make sustaining and secure to the English
race. But the Spaniards, accustomed in America
to living off the supplies and labor of submissive
natives, were not allured by the prospect of taming
tall Creek warriors, or of tilling the soil and hunting game to maintain themselves in the wilderness.
They had astounding enterprise and courage for
any rainbow trail that promised a pot of gold at the
end of it, but little for manual labor.

When news of Villafañe's failure reached Spain,
Philip decided against any further attempts to
colonize Florida for the time being. He was reassured, as to France, because the French as yet
had not made any firm foothold on American soil.
There seemed little to alarm him in the steady
increase of their fishing vessels, alongside those of
Spain, in Newfoundland waters, or in the small
trade in the furs the fishermen were bringing home
yearly. He could not foresee that not the pot of
gold but the beaver was to lead to the solution of

the Northern Mystery and to spread colonies from
the Atlantic to the Pacific. Moreover, thought
the King, where Spaniards had failed, Frenchmen could not succeed. So, in September, 1561,
Philip issued his declaration with regard to the
northern coast. It is interesting to note that he was
largely influenced to this decision by the advice of
Pedro Menéndez de Avilés, who was very shortly
to change both his own mind and Philip's. But no
doubt he relied more on the treaty signed in 1559
between himself and Henry II of France, under
which France surrendered booty from Spanish
ships and ports, said — perhaps somewhat extrava-
gantly — to equal in value a third of the kingdom;
and on his own marriage by proxy in the same
year to the French princess Elizabeth, daughter of
Catherine de' Medici.

But Philip's policy of hands off Florida was destined to speedy reversal, to meet the exigency of
a new intrusion into Spanish domains. A year
had not passed when Jean Ribaut of Dieppe led a
colony of French Huguenots to Port Royal, South
Carolina, the very Santa Elena which Villafañe,
less than a year before, had tried to occupy for
Spain. Ribaut's enterprise dismally failed, it is
true, but two years later Coligny, Admiral of

France, a Huguenot, and the uncompromising foe of Spain, sent a second colony under René de Laudonnière. And a French settlement was founded, protected by Fort Caroline, on St. John's River, in the land of which Ponce de León had taken solemn possession for Spain.

The enthusiastic reports made by these French pioneers are proof that not alone the Spanish fancy ran astray in the face of tales that were told in the American wilds. Ribaut heard of the Seven Cities of Cíbola; but Laudonnière went him one better, for one of his scouts, while exploring the country round about, actually saw and conversed with men who had drunk at the Fountain of Youth, and had already comfortably passed their first quarter of a thousand years.

But Laudonnière's artistic sense did not fit him to lead a colony made up chiefly of ex-soldiers — and including both Huguenots and Catholics, who had so recently been in armed strife on their home soil. Men who tilled the ground had been omitted from the roster; the artisans could not turn farmers on the instant; and the soldiers had no inclination to beat their swords into plowshares so long as Spanish treasure ships sailed the Bahama Channel. Laudonnière offended the Indians nearby by

trying to make friends with their foes as well and
forcing them to set free some captives, and so was
presently in straits for food. Some of his men
mutinied, seized two barques, and went out on a
pirate raid. One of their vessels with thirty-three
men aboard was captured by the Spaniards and
the men hanged — in return for their seizure of a
Spanish ship and the killing of a judge aboard of
her. The other barque returned to Fort Caroline
and Laudonnière had the ringleaders executed.
Only ten days' supply of food was left, when one
morning, like gulls rising against the sun, four
strange sails fluttered over the horizon. Instead of
Spaniards bent on war, the visitor, who sailed his
fleet into the river's mouth, proved to be the
English sea-dog, John Hawkins. Master Hawkins had been marketing a cargo of Guinea Coast
blacks in the islands where, by a suggestive display of swords and arquebuses, he had forced the
Spaniards to meet his prices and to give him
a "testimoniall of his good behauior" while in
their ports.

Hawkins fed and wined the French settlers and
offered to carry them away safely to French soil.
But Laudonnière, not knowing whether France
was at peace or war with England, was afraid to

trust the generous pirate. So far from resenting Laudonnière's suspicions, Hawkins, no doubt thinking that, in like circumstances, he would be equally cautious, agreed to sell a vessel at whatever price the Frenchman should name. And he threw into the bargain provisions and fifty pairs of shoes, so that Laudonnière, in his memoir, descants much upon this "good and charitable man."

Grave reports of Laudonnière's mismanagement reached Coligny and decided him to send Jean Ribaut again to take command. Ribaut, with his son Jacques and three hundred more colonists, chiefly soldiers, set sail on May 23, 1565. On the eve of departure Ribaut received a letter from Coligny, saying that a certain Don Pedro Menéndez was leaving Spain for the coast of "New France" — such the French declared to be the name of the coast south of the St. Lawrence. Coligny sternly counseled Ribaut not to suffer Menéndez to "encroach" upon him "no more than he would that you should encroach upon him."

If the settlement at Port Royal had been a disquieting intrusion, Fort Caroline, under the very nose of Havana and on the path of the treasure fleets, was an imminent menace to New Spain. Its import was plainly stated in the reports to

Philip from Mexico. "The sum of all that can be said in the matter, is that they put the Indies in a crucible, for we are compelled to pass in front of their port, and with the greatest ease they can sally out with their armadas to seek us, and easily return home when it suits them." In urging action before Coligny could send Ribaut to relieve the colonists, the same report continued: "seeing that they are Lutherans . . . it is not needful to leave a man alive, but to inflict an exemplary punishment, that they may remember it forever."[1] While French depredations had been protested by Philip's envoy to France, the matter had not been pushed to a rupture, because Philip desired to enlist the aid of Catherine. Catherine also was forced to temporize. She needed Philip's support to maintain her position of power in France between Catholic Leaguer and Huguenot, but she dared not, for his friendship, go so far as to interfere with Coligny's designs on Florida, lest even the French Catholics turn against her; for they too had caught the Admiral's vision of a France once more great, rich, and glorious. It suited her therefore to make answer that the French ships were bound for a country discovered by France and known as

[1] Lowery, *Florida*, p. 105.

the *Terre des Bretons* and would in no way molest the territories of Spain!

Ribaut reached Fort Caroline while Laudonnière and his men were still there. With the arrival of his ships, bringing three hundred more colonists, plans for evacuation were abandoned.

To expel and castigate the French and to plant his own power solidly in Florida, Philip had at last picked a man who would not fail. Menéndez was already a sea-soldier of note and had rendered signal and distinguished services to the Crown. He was a nobleman of the Asturias, where "the earth and sky bear men who are honest, not tricksters, truthful, not babblers, most faithful to the King, generous, friendly, light-hearted, and merry, daring, and warlike." During the recent wars, as a naval officer, he had fought the French; and later, off his home coasts and off the Canaries, he had defeated French pirate ships.

Menéndez's contract was a typical conquistador's agreement. His chance to serve the King was a certainty. His profits were a gamble. The title of *adelantado* of Florida granted him was made hereditary. His salary of two thousand ducats yearly was to be collected from rents and products of the colony. He was given a grant of land twenty-five miles square, with the title of Marquis, and two fisheries — one of pearls — wherever he should select them. He was to have a few ships of his own to trade with some of the islands and was absolved from certain import and export duties, and for five years he was to retain whatever spoils he found aboard the pirate vessels he captured. Apart from a loan from Philip of fifteen thousand ducats, which he bound himself to repay, he was to bear all the expenses of the venture — about $1,800,000. His fleet was to contain, besides the *San Pelayo* of six hundred tons, six sloops of fifty tons each and four smaller vessels for use in the shallow waters of Florida. His colonists were to number five hundred, of which one hundred must be soldiers, one hundred sailors, and the rest artisans, officials, and farmers; and two hundred of them must be married. He was to take four Jesuit priests and ten or twelve friars. He was to parcel out the land to settlers and to build two towns, each to contain one hundred citizens and to be protected by a fort. He was also to take about five hundred negro slaves, half of whom were to be women. Above all he was to see that none of his colonists were Jews or secret heretics. And he was to drive out the French settlers "by what means you see fit." He must also make a detailed report on the Atlantic coast from the Florida Keys to Newfoundland. The previous success of Menéndez as a chastiser of pirates may be indicated by his possession of nearly two million dollars to spend on this colony. When his entire company was raised, it comprised 2646 persons, "not mendicants and vagabonds . . . but of the best horsemen of Asturias, Galicia, and Vizcaya," "trustworthy persons, for the security of the enterprise."

Menéndez sailed from Cádiz on July 29, 1565. In the islands thirty of his men and three priests deserted; but neither this circumstance nor the non-arrival of half his ships, which were delayed by storms, prevented him from continuing at once for Florida. On the 28th of August he dropped anchor in a harbor about the mouth of a river and gave to it the name of the saint on whose festival he had discovered it — Saint Augustine (San Agustín).

Seven days later he went up the coast, looking for the French. In the afternoon he came upon four of Ribaut's ships lying outside the bar at St. John's River. Menéndez, ignoring the French fire, which was aimed too high to do any damage, led his vessels in among the foe's.

"Gentlemen, from where does this fleet come?" he demanded, as we are told, "very courteously."

"From France," came the answer from Ribaut's flagship.

"What are you doing here?"

"Bringing infantry, artillery, and supplies for a fort which the King of France has in this country, and for others which he is going to make."

"Are you Catholics or Lutherans?"

"Lutherans, and our general is Jean Ribaut."

In answer to like questions from the French ship, Menéndez made reply: "I am the General; my name is Pedro Menéndez de Avilés. This is the armada of the King of Spain, who has sent me to this coast and country to burn and hang the Lutheran French who should be found there, and in the morning I will board your ships; and if I find any Catholics they will be well treated."[1]

In the pause which followed this exchange of courtesies — "a stillness such as I have never heard since I came to the world," says the Spanish chaplain — the French cut their cables and, passing through the midst of the Spanish fleet, made off to sea. Menéndez gave chase. But the French

[1] This conversation is quoted by Lowery in *Florida*, pp. 156–157.

ships were too swift for him. So at dawn he returned to the river's mouth. But, seeing the three other French vessels within the bar and soldiers massed on the bank, he withdrew and sailed back to St. Augustine. Here he began the fortification of a large Indian house, dug a trench about it, and bulwarked it with logs and earth. This converted Indian dwelling was the beginning of the settlement of St. Augustine. The work finished and the last of the colonists and supplies landed, Menéndez took formal possession. From a distance the French ships watched the landing of the Spanish troops; then made off to St. John's River.

On arrival at Fort Caroline Ribaut gathered his vessels together — except his son's, which had not returned — and, taking aboard four hundred soldiers, set out again, to attack St. Augustine. He left only two hundred and forty men at Fort Caroline; and many of them were ill. His plans were made against the advice of Laudonnière, left in command of the fort, who urged the danger of his situation should contrary winds drive Ribaut's ships out to sea and the Spaniards make an attack by land. These forebodings were prophetic. A terrible wind arose which blew for days. And Menéndez, guided by Indians and a French

prisoner he had picked up in the islands, marched
overland upon Fort Caroline.

On the 20th of September just before daybreak
Menéndez reached the fort. Most of the men
inside were asleep. The trumpeter on the bastion
had barely sounded the alarm before the Spaniards
were inside the walls. The French had no time
to don clothes or armor. In their shirts or naked
they seized their swords and rushed out into the
gray light of the court. Within an hour one
hundred and thirty-two French had been killed,
and half a dozen men and fifty women and children
captured. The remaining French, many of them
wounded, escaped to the woods; among them was
Laudonnière. It was not a fight but a massacre.
Even the very sick were dragged out and slain.
One woman who escaped had a dagger wound in
her breast; though Menéndez had given orders to
spare the women and children, fearing "that our
Lord would punish me, if I acted towards them
with cruelty."

Twenty-six French, including Laudonnière, were
rescued by the ships of Jacques Ribaut and ultimately reached France. Some twenty more, too
badly hurt to travel fast, were discovered by the
men sent out by Menéndez to beat the brush

thoroughly for fugitives and run through with swords. One lone man, a belated Cabeza de Vaca, made his way across the country from tribe to tribe and came out at Pánuco. After a brief rest at the post, which he rechristened Fort San Mateo, Menéndez marched swiftly back to St. Augustine. He learned presently that one hundred and forty men from two French ships wrecked by the storm were nearby. They had lost two hundred of their comrades, drowned, killed, or captured by savages; they themselves were destitute. Menéndez made a quick march to the spot. When the castaways pleaded that their lives be spared until the arrival of a French ship to take them home, Menéndez answered that he was "waging a war of fire and blood against all who came to settle these parts and plant in them their evil Lutheran sect. . . . For this reason I would not grant them a safe passage, but would sooner follow them by sea and land until I had taken their lives." [1]

An offer of five thousand ducats for their lives met with the ambiguous reply that mercy would be shown for its own sake and not for price. So read the Spanish reports of this event. French reports state that Menéndez, to induce the one

[1] Ruidiaz, *La Florida*, vol. II, p. 89.

hundred and forty men to surrender themselves, their arms, and ammunition without a blow, gave his oath to spare their lives and to send them to France.   However that may be, they surrendered. The chaplain discovered ten Catholics among them and these were set apart.   The remaining one hundred and thirty were given food and drink and were then told that — as a precaution because of their numbers — they must consent to have their hands bound behind them on the march to St. Augustine. Menéndez ordered a meal prepared for the prisoners, gave his final instructions regarding them to the officers in charge, and went on ahead.   A gunshot's distance off, beyond a hummock, he paused long enough to draw a line with his spear in the white sand of the flat.   Then he went on. The heavy dusk from the sea was massing swiftly behind the Frenchmen, and the last faint flush of the afterglow was fading from the western sky, when they came up abreast of the spear-line in the sand.   There the Spaniards fell upon them, slew, and decapitated them.   The stain on the ground where this bloody scene was enacted is ineradicable, and after three and a half centuries the place is still known as Las Matanzas (The Massacre).

Shortly after Menéndez had reached St. Augustine, Indians informed him that Jean Ribaut and two hundred men were at Matanzas, having been cut off there, as the other Frenchmen had been, by the inlet, as they were attempting to reach Fort Caroline by land.   Menéndez set out immediately. Once more were the same ceremonies repeated; and Ribaut and his two hundred men were induced to surrender.   When, with their hands bound, they were halted at the spear-line, now more clearly indicated by the heap of corpses along it, they were asked: "Are you Catholics or Lutherans, and are there any who wish to confess?"   Seventeen Catholics were found and set aside.   But Ribaut, the staunch Huguenot mariner of Dieppe, had been too long familiar with the menace of death to recant because a dagger was poised over his entrails.   He answered for himself and the rest, saying that a score of years of life were a small matter, for "from earth we came and unto earth we return."   Then he recited passages from Psalm cxxxii.   One of Menéndez's captains thrust his dagger into Ribaut's bowels, and Merás, the *adelantado's* brother-in-law, drove his pike through his breast; then they hacked off his head.

"I put Jean Ribaut and all the rest of them to the

knife," Menéndez wrote to Philip, "judging it to be necessary to the service of the Lord Our God, and of Your Majesty. And I think it a very great fortune that this man be dead . . . he could do more in one year than another in ten; for he was the most experienced sailor and corsair known, very skillful in this navigation of the Indies and of the Florida Coast."[1]

Some there were, of course, among his officers at St. Augustine, and among the nobility in Spain, who condemned Menéndez for his cruelty and for slaying the captives after having given his oath for their safety. But Barrientos, a contemporary historian, holds that he was "very merciful" to them for he could "legally have burnt them alive . . . He killed them, I think, rather by divine inspiration." And Philip's comment, scribbled by his pen on the back of Menéndez's dispatch, was: "As to those he has killed he has done well, and as to those he has saved, they shall be sent to the galleys."[2] And he wrote to Menéndez, "We hold that we have been well served."

The name of Menéndez is popularly associated in America almost solely with this inhuman episode. But the expulsion of the French was only an

[1] Lowery, *Florida*, p. 200.   [2] Lowery, *Florida*, p. 206

incident in a work covering nearly ten years, during which time Menéndez proved himself an able and constructive administrator, as well as a vigorous soldier, and laid the foundation of a Spanish colony on the northern mainland which endured.

Menéndez was a dreamer, as are all men of vision, and he pictured a great future for his Florida — which to him meant the whole of northeastern America. He would fortify the Peninsula to prevent any foreigner from gaining control of the Bahama Channel, that highway of the precious treasure fleets; he would ascend the Atlantic coast and occupy Santa Elena, where the French had intruded, and the Bay of Santa María (Chesapeake Bay), for, since one of its arms was perhaps the long-sought northern passage, the bay might prove to be the highway to the Moluccas, much endangered now by the activities of the French. The other extremity, on the Pacific, it was hoped, might be discovered by Legazpi, who shortly before had started on his way to conquer the Philippine Islands. This accomplished, then away with France and her Bacallaos (St. Lawrence) River, which, after all, Cartier and Roberval had found untenable. To approach Mexico, Menéndez would occupy Appalachee Bay, and plant a colony at

Coosa, "at the foot of the mountains which come from the mines of Zacatecas and San Martín," where Francisco de Ibarra was at this very moment engaged in carving out the Kingdom of New Biscay. Finally, Menéndez had great hopes of economic prosperity, for silkworms, vineyards, mines, pearls, sugar plantations, wheat and rice fields, herds of cattle, salines, ship timber, and pitch would make Florida not only self-supporting but richer "than New Spain or even Peru."

Vast and unified in vision were these contemporaneous projects of Philip and his men, embracing the two oceans and reaching from Spain to the Philippine Islands. The tasks of Menéndez in La Florida, Ibarra in New Biscay, and Legaspi in the Philippines were all but parts of one great whole, and Florida, said Menéndez, with a twentieth-century contempt for distance and a Spanish disregard of time, "is but a suburb of Spain, for it does not take more than forty days' sailing to come here, and usually as many more to return."

Within two years Menéndez had established a line of posts between Tampa Bay and Santa Elena (Port Royal) and had made an attempt to colonize Virginia. But this work had not been done without setbacks. Disease and the adventurer's

dislike of manual labor — the same enemies that
so nearly wrecked the English settlement at Jamestown several decades later — played their part in
hampering the growth of the Florida settlements.
When the colonies might perhaps have been in a
degree self-supporting, it was still necessary to
import all their supplies. Over a hundred colonists
died at St. Augustine and San Mateo (Fort Caroline); the attitude of others was fairly expressed
in the statement of some deserters, that they had
not come there to plow and plant but to find
riches and, since no riches were to be found, they
would no longer live in Florida "like beasts."
From the principal settlements over three hundred
men absconded; one hundred and thirty belonging
to St. Augustine seized a supply ship and made off
in it. But Menéndez's forces were strengthened
by over a thousand colonists from Spain. The
foothold in Florida had been won.

Meanwhile Menéndez had turned to inland
exploration. While at Santa Elena in 1566, he
sent Juan Pardo with twenty-five men "to discover and conquer the interior country from
there to Mexico." Menéndez aimed to join
hands with the advance guard of pioneers in
New Biscay. Going northward through Orista-

at forty leagues Pardo apparently struck the Cambahee River. Turning west he visited Cufitachiqui, where De Soto had dallied with the "queen" a quarter century before. A few days later he was at Juala, on a stream near the foot of the Alleghanies. The mountain being covered with snow, he could not proceed, so he built a stockade, called Fort San Juan, and left there a garrison under Sergeant Boyano. Going east to Guataré (Wateree), he left there a priest and four soldiers, and returned by a direct route to Santa Elena. He had thus extended the work of De Soto by exploring a large part of South Carolina and adding considerably to the knowledge of North Carolina.

Conversion of the natives was an essential part of Menéndez's scheme to pacify and hold the country. He had, as yet, no missionaries; so he detailed some of his soldiers to the work, and, in 1566, by much urging, he induced Philip to equip and send three Jesuits to Florida. The three were Father Martínez, Father Rogel, and Brother Villareal. Their mission began in disaster. Father Martínez was killed by Indians and the other two withdrew temporarily to the West Indies. On their return, Menéndez established Father Rogel with a garrison of fifty soldiers at San Antonio, on Charlotte Bay, in the territory of the cacique Carlos, and Brother Villareal, also with a garrison, at Tegesta on the Miami River mouth at Biscayne Bay.

Menéndez had now established three permanent settlements on the Atlantic coast — St. Augustine and San Mateo in Florida and Santa Elena in South Carolina; and he had garrisoned forts at Guale in northern Georgia, at Tampa and Charlotte Bays on the west coast of the peninsula, and at Biscayne Bay and the St. Lucie River on the east coast. From these points Spaniards would now command the routes of the treasure fleets from the West Indies and from Vera Cruz. He had also projected a settlement at Chesapeake Bay, which was not fated to endure.

In May, 1567, after twenty months of continuous activity, Menéndez went to Spain. There he was acclaimed as a hero. Philip made him Captain-General of the West, with command of a large fleet to secure the route to the West Indies, appointed him Governor of Cuba, and created him Knight Commander of the Holy Cross of Zarza, of the order of Santiago. It was said that Menéndez was greatly disappointed that his reward consisted of so many sonorous words and of so little substance.

Menéndez had reached his zenith. The story of his later successes is varied with disasters.

In France, among all parties, the news of the massacre of Ribaut's colony had kindled fury against the Spaniards. Even to Catherine, in that hour of humiliation, the slaughtered men in Florida were not Huguenots but French. She rejected Philip's insinuating suggestions to make Coligny the scapegoat, avowed her own responsibility, and protested bitterly the effrontery and cruelty of Philip's agent in murdering her subjects. But her position in divided France was such that Philip had the whip hand, and he couched his answers in terms to make her feel it. She dared not go beyond high words, lest he publish her as an enemy of her own Church and, by some sudden stroke at her or her invalid son, hasten the end at which all his intrigues in her kingdom aimed, namely, the complete subservience of France to the Spanish Crown.

Catherine could not avenge the wrong; but Dominique de Gourgues could. Gourgues was an ex-soldier and a citizen of good family; his parents were Catholics and he is not known to have been a Protestant. He had been captured in war by the Spaniards and had been forced

to serve as a galley slave.   Now to his own
grievance was added that of his nation; and he
chose to avenge both.   It is possible that he did
not have the aid of the Queen and Coligny in
raising his expedition — ostensibly to engage in
the slave trade — but quite probable that he did.
He timed his stroke to fall during the absence of
Menéndez in Spain.   With one hundred and eighty
men he went out in August, 1567, and spent the
winter trading in the West Indies.   Early next year
he proceeded to Florida, landed quietly near St.
John's River and made an alliance with Chief
Saturiba, who was hostile to the Spaniards but an
old friend of the French.   Saturiba received him
with demonstrations of joy, called his secondary
chiefs to a war council, and presented Gourgues
with a French lad whom his tribe had succored
and concealed from the Spaniards since the time
of Ribaut.

His force augmented by Saturiba's warriors,
Gourgues marched stealthily upon San Mateo.
The Spaniards in the outpost blockhouses had
just dined "and were still picking their teeth"
when Gourgues's cry rang out:

"Yonder are the thieves who have stolen this
land from our King.   Yonder are the murderers

who have massacred our French. On! On! Let us avenge our King! Let us show that we are Frenchmen!"

The garrison in the first blockhouse, sixty in all, were killed or captured. The men in the second blockhouse met the same fate; and the French pushed on towards San Mateo fort itself, their fury having been increased by the sight of French cannon on the blockhouses — reminders of Fort Caroline. The Spaniards at San Mateo had received warning. A number had made off towards St. Augustine; the remaining garrison opened artillery fire upon the French. The trees screened the Indian allies; and the Spaniards, in making a sortie, were caught between the two forces. "As many as possible were taken alive, by Captain Gourgues's order, to do to them what they had done to the French," says the report. The completion of Gourgues's revenge is thus related: "They are swung from the branches of the same trees on which they had hung the French, and in place of the inscription which Pedro Menéndez had put up containing these words in Spanish, *I do this not as to Frenchmen but as to Lutherans*, Captain Gourgues causes to be inscribed with a hot iron on a pine tablet: *I do this not as to*

*Spaniards nor as to Marranos [secret Jews] but as
to traitors, robbers, and murderers."* [1]

Gourgues now turned homeward. On the way
he captured three Spanish treasure ships, threw
their crews overboard, and took their contents of
gold, pearls, merchandise, and arms. With a
hideous vindictiveness on land and water had he
repaid Spaniards for the massacre of his countrymen on Florida soil and for his own degradation
as a slave in their galleys on the sea. And he,
too, like Menéndez, stepping red-handed upon his
native shores, was acclaimed as a hero.

Troubles now came fast upon the Spaniards in
Florida. Indians rose and massacred the soldiers
at Tampa Bay. The garrison at San Antonio was
compelled by hunger and the hostility of the natives to withdraw to St. Augustine. In rapid succession, the interior posts established by Pardo
and Boyano were destroyed by the Indians, or
abandoned to save provisions. By 1570 Indian
rancor and shortage of food had forced numbers of
the colonists to leave the country.

[1] Lowery, *Florida*, p. 333. There seems to be no proof that
Menéndez had hanged Frenchmen at Fort Caroline with this
inscription over them; but the report that he had done so was
believed in France. Spanish accounts do not mention it.

The missionaries succeeded little better than the soldiers; though Menéndez had sent out fourteen more Jesuits from Spain, in 1568, under Father Juan Bautista de Segura. Father Rogel, driven from San Antonio and then from Santa Elena, returned to Havana. Father Sedeño and some five companions went to Guale (Georgia) where they labored for a year with some success. Brother Domingo translated the catechism into the native Guale tongue and Brother Baez compiled a grammar, the first written in the United States. Father Rogel went to Santa Elena, where he founded a mission at Orista, some five leagues from the settlement of San Felipe. He succeeded well for several months, but finally the Indians became hostile and, when the commander levied a tribute of provisions to feed the hungry settlers, they rebelled, and Father Rogel was forced to withdraw to Havana (1570). About the same time and for like reasons the missionaries abandoned Guale.

Though he had failed on the peninsula and on the coasts of Georgia and South Carolina, Father Segura did not give up, but transferred his efforts to Chesapeake Bay, where, with six other Jesuits, he founded a mission at Axacan, perhaps on the Rappahannock. But within a few months the fickle Indians turned against them and slew Segura and his entire band (1571). On his return from Spain Menéndez went to Chesapeake Bay and avenged the death of the missionaries by hanging eight Indians to the yardarms of his ship.

The Jesuits, after the martyrdom of Segura, abandoned the field of Florida for Mexico. But, in 1573, nine Franciscans began work in this unpromising territory. Others came in 1577 and, in 1593, twelve more arrived under Father Juan de Silva. From their monastery at St. Augustine they set forth and founded missions along the northern coasts. Fray Pedro Chozas made wide explorations inland; and Father Pareja began his famous work on the Indian languages. By 1615 more than twenty mission stations were erected in the region today comprised in Florida, Georgia, and South Carolina. The story of these Franciscan missions, though it is little known, is one of self-sacrifice, religious zeal, and heroism, scarcely excelled by that of the Jesuits in Canada or the Franciscans in California. It is recorded in the mute but eloquent ruins scattered here and there along the Atlantic coast.

In 1572 Menéndez left America. He was first of all a seaman; and he was called home to assist

Philip in the preparation of the great Armada which the King was slowly getting ready. But Menéndez did not live to command the Armada, for he died in 1574. His body was carried to the Church of St. Nicholas in Avilés and placed in a niche on the Gospel side of the altar. His tomb is marked with this inscription: "Here lies interred the very illustrious cavalier Pedro Men^z de Avilés, native of this town, Adelantado of the Provinces of Florida, Commander of the Holy Cross of La Çarça of the Order of Santiago and Cⁿ Gen^{al} of the Ocean Sea and of the Catholic Armada which the Lord Philip II. assembled against England in the year 1574, at Santander, where he died on the 17th of September of the said year being fifty-five years of age."[1]

At the time when Menéndez returned to Spain, Philip's intrigues in France reached their logical culmination — in the Massacre of St. Bartholomew and the end of Coligny. France, again in the agonies of civil strife, was no longer a menace. The new shadow on his horizon was England — England with her growing navy and her Protestant faith: and her Queen, who was as expert a politician as

[1] Lowery, *Florida*, p. 384.

any man sent by Spain to her court, and more subtle then Philip himself. "This woman is possessed by a hundred thousand devils," the Spanish envoy wrote to his King. During the years while England, after the upheavals of Mary's reign, was becoming stable and waxing strong, Elizabeth's dexterity kept Philip halting from any one of the deadly blows he might have struck at her. By her brilliant wit and her mendacity she kept him pondering when he should have been acting. She worked upon his religious zeal and his vanity by letting herself be surprised by his envoy with a crucifix in her hands, or blushing with a pretty confusion over Philip's portraits; and by these and other methods she kept him from bringing his intrigues among her Catholic subjects to a head, lessened his support of Mary Stuart, and caused him to put off his designs for her own assassination. But this play could not go on forever. The piracies of the English sea-dogs, the honoring by Elizabeth of Francis Drake on his return from looting Spanish ships and "taking possession" of the North Pacific coast as New Albion, the attempts of Raleigh and White to plant colonies in Virginia and Guiana, and later the sacking of Santo Domingo and Cartagena and the destruction of

St. Augustine by Drake, and, finally, the persecu-
tion of the Jesuits in England, at last spurred Philip
to combat.   By the Pope, who had issued a Bull of
Deposition against Elizabeth, he had long been
urged to conquer renegade England; and Mary
Stuart had bequeathed to him her "rights" as
sovereign of that kingdom.   And Philip had seen
that his distant colonies could not be defended
unless he were sole King of the Ocean Sea.

So the destiny of North America was decided
on the North Sea, in July, 1588, in the defeat of
the Spanish Armada by Sir Francis Drake.   The
mastery of the ocean passed from Spain to England.
The waterways were open now for English colonists to seek those northern shores which Spain
had failed to occupy.   In time the sparse settlements in the Spanish province of Florida came to
be hemmed in on the north by the English colonies in Georgia and South Carolina and Alabama,
and stopped on the west by the French colony
of Louisiana.

Jamestown, 1607; Charleston, 1670; Savannah,
1733: thus the English advanced relentlessly.   And
in 1763, following the Seven Years' War, in which
Spain fought on the side of France, the English
expelled Spain from Florida entirely.   Spain's

recovery of her foothold there during the American Revolution, and her struggle afterwards to hold back the oncoming tide of the now independent Anglo-Americans, profited her nothing in the end; for in 1819, two hundred and twelve years after Jamestown, all that remained to Spain of her old province of Florida passed to the United States.

CHAPTER VI

NEW MEXICO

OLD Castañeda, who wrote a belated chronicle of Coronado's expedition, gave Coronado a black eye and at the same time encouraged new flights of fancy. He made it appear that for some man of destiny the north held prizes. From the resemblance of the Pueblo to the Aztec dwellings the region came to be called New Mexico. It was, after all, the "otro Mexico," which so many had sought. For nearly four decades after Coronado's day the Pueblo Indians were not revisited; but, during the interval the frontier of settlement in the central plateau of Mexico pushed northward, and the post of Santa Bárbara was set up at the head of the Conchos River, which led to the Río Grande. This opened a new highway to New Mexico. Coronado's roundabout trail by way of the Pacific slope, made dangerous by hostile Indians using poisoned arrows, was now no longer necessary. In the course of slave-catching and prospecting raids down the Conchos, frontiersmen crossed the trail of Cabeza de Vaca and from the Indians heard new reports of the Pueblo country. Some one at Santa Bárbara had a copy of Vaca's *Narrative*, and the marvelous tale of adventure was read again with keen attention. To the friars, newly heralded Cíbola appeared a virgin field in which to save souls; to the soldiers and miners, a new world of adventure and treasure.

New Mexico was again the scene of exploration. But, by the ordinance of 1573, military expeditions among the Indians were forbidden, and as a consequence any new enterprise must go in missionary guise. An expedition was organized at Santa Bárbara in 1581, led by Fray Agustín Rodriguez, with whom went Fray Francisco López, Fray Juan de Santa Maria, nineteen Indian servants, and nine soldier-traders. The soldiers were led by Francisco Chamuscado, "the Singed." They were equipped with ninety horses, coats of mail for horse and rider, and six hundred cattle, besides sheep, goats, and hogs. For barter with the natives they carried merchandise. While the primary purpose of the stock was to provide **food on** the way, the friars were prepared to remain in New Mexico if conditions were propitious.

Leaving Santa Bárbara on the 5th of June, the party descended the Conchos River to its mouth and proceeded up the Río Grande. They were followed by a retinue of Indians who regarded them as children of the sun — so the chronicler thought. They passed through the Piros towns and continued to the Tiguas above Isleta, and on to the Tanos on Santa Fé River. Here Father Santa María set out alone to carry reports to Mexico, against the wishes of his companions, whose fears were justified, for he was killed three days later by Indians east of Isleta. The two friars and their party continued to Taos, near the Colorado line, and crossed to the Buffalo Plains, east of the Pecos River. Returning westward, they were obliged to fight a band of hostile natives in the Galisteo valley. Then they crossed the Río Grande and visited the Indian towns of Ácoma and Zuñi. On the way some of the men, boylike, or with an historical sense, carved their names on El Morro Cliff, now called Inscription Rock, where they are still visible. At Zuñi they found three Mexicans who had come with Coronado, and after forty years had nearly forgotten their native tongue. Back eastward came the

expedition. Rodriguez and López decided to found
a mission at Puaray, a Tigua town on the Río
Grande above Albuquerque, and there, with a few
servants, the two friars made their abode. The
soldiers returned to Santa Bárbara. Chamuscado,
the leader, became ill on the way and was carried
on a litter of hides strung between two horses.
Before reaching his destination he died.

Three months later two servants from the mission fled to Mexico and reported that López had
been killed by the Indians. A rescue expedition
was hastened, for Fray Agustín might still be
alive. But the expedition was too late. On reaching Puaray it was learned that Fray Agustín also
had been slain.

The soldier-traders of this rescue party were led
by Antonio de Espejo, a merchant of Mexico, and
Espejo had other business in New Mexico. From
the Río Grande he explored northwest to Jémez
and went to Ácoma and Zuñi. Here he left Father
Beltrán, the Franciscan who accompanied him, and
went on in search of a lake of gold he had heard
of. Arrived at the Moqui towns, in Arizona, he
obtained four thousand cotton blankets and saw
the snake dance performed by the Hopi Indians,
who still raise cotton and still perform the famous

dance, usually as a prayer for rain. Espejo now pushed westward and reached the region of Prescott, where he discovered rich veins, later to be known as mines of fabulous wealth. Then, retracing his steps to the Río Grande, he returned by way of the Pecos River to Santa Bárbara, whither Father Beltrán had preceded him. Espejo's report of the mines, of course, set the frontier on fire.

The rumor that Drake, after raiding Spanish ships on the Pacific (1579), had found the Strait of Anian, and had sailed home through it, impelled the Spaniards to extend their power northward to the shores of that Strait. So Philip ordered the Viceroy of Mexico to make a contract with some one for the conquest and settlement of New Mexico. Several applicants came forward, including Espejo, who proposed at his own expense to colonize New Mexico with four hundred soldier-settlers and to build a port where the Strait of Anian entered the North Sea! So great was the excitement in Mexico that some adventurers did not wait for official sanction, but set out on their own authority, knowing that nothing succeeds like success. No result came of these unauthorized ventures, and, what with red tape and jealousies and disputes, it was some years before a contract was concluded with any one. The King had his Armada on his mind and, for the time, was pinning all his hopes upon that. But, in 1588, his Armada was beaten and almost wholly destroyed. His command of the sea was gone. And he turned again to his subjects in Mexico for help to make his power in the New World secure. At last, in 1595, just when Vizcaíno was commissioned to colonize and hold California, the contract for the conquest and settlement of New Mexico was awarded to Juan de Oñate of Zacatecas. The two expeditions, indeed, were regarded as parts of the same enterprise.

Oñate was the scion of a family distinguished for generations through service to the Crown in Spain and in Mexico; and he had married Isabel Tolosa Cortés Montezuma, a descendant of both Cortés and Montezuma II. He was granted extensive privileges in New Mexico, much like those conferred upon Menéndez in Florida thirty years before. His colonists were promised the rank of hidalgo — for themselves and their heirs. The expedition was prepared in feudal style. Men of means were made captains. They did homage and swore fealty to Oñate, sounded fife and drum, set up standards, and raised companies at their own expense. Rich men staked their fortunes on the gamble.

Zacatecas was made the central rendezvous for the colony, which was recruited from far and near. Jealousies and underminings interfered so much in the preliminary stages that it was 1598 before Oñate left Santa Bárbara, the last important outpost on the frontier. In his train went one hundred and thirty soldier-settlers, most of them taking their families, a band of Franciscans under Father Martínez, a large retinue of negro and Indian slaves, seven thousand head of stock, and eighty-three wagons and carts for transporting the women and children and the baggage.

The baggage must have been ample indeed if all the officers were as well supplied as Captain Luís de Velasco with wardrobe and appurtenances suitable to a cavalier in the wilderness. Don Luís had one suit of "blue Italian velvet trimmed with wide gold passementerie, consisting of doublet, breeches, and green silk stockings with blue garters and points of gold lace," a suit of rose satin, one of straw-colored satin, another of purple Castilian cloth, another of chestnut colored cloth, a sixth and daintier one, of Chinese flowered silk. He had two doublets of Castilian dressed kid and one of royal lion skin gold-trimmed; two linen shirts, fourteen pairs of Rouen linen breeches, forty pairs of boots, shoes, and gaiters, three hats, one black, trimmed around the crown with a silver cord and black, purple, and white feathers, another gray with yellow and purple feathers, the third of purple taffeta trimmed with blue, purple, and yellow feathers and a band of gold and silver passementerie. He took four saddles "of blue flowered Spanish cloth bound with Cordovan leather," three suits of armor, and three suits of horse armor, a silver-handled lance with gold and purple tassels, a sword and gilded dagger with belts stitched in purple and yellow silk, a broadsword, two shields, and — as a protection against weather and sneezes — a raincoat and six linen handkerchiefs. A bedstead and two mattresses with coverlet, sheets, pillows, and pillow-cases and a canvas mattress-bag bound with leather completed his outfit — not forgetting servants, thirty horses and mules, and a silken banner.

Instead of continuing down the Conchos, Oñate opened a new trail direct to the Río Grande. Early in April (1598) he reached the Médanos, the great sand dunes south of El Paso. On the twenty-sixth he camped on the river just below El Paso. Here on the thirtieth he took formal possession "of all the Kingdoms and provinces of New Mexico, on the Río del Norte, in the name of our Lord King Philip." The day was given up to a celebration beginning with artillery salutes, Mass, and a sermon, and concluding with the presentation of a comedy written by Captain Farfán. On the 4th of May Oñate crossed the Río Grande at El Paso. Then with sixty men he went ahead in person "to pacify the land." Two months later, at the present Santo Domingo, a pueblo west of Santa Fé, he received the submission of the chiefs of seven provinces. Continuing north a short distance, on July 11, 1598, he established headquarters at the pueblo of Caypa, then renamed and ever since known as San Juan. With the aid of fifteen hundred natives he began the construction of an irrigation ditch. His colonists came up with him early in August; and, on the 8th of September, they celebrated the completion of the first church erected in New Mexico. On the next day chiefs from all the explored territory assembled to do honor to their Spanish super-chief and to receive their rods of office as lieutenants of King Philip. A tone of solemnity was given the scene by holding the ceremony in the kiva, or sacred council chamber, of the pueblo. There, on bended knee, the chiefs swore allegiance to God and the King of Spain, and sealed the oath by kissing the hands of Oñate and Father Martínez.

The ceremony over, Oñate gave his mind to plans for exploration. He wished to explore the Buffalo Plains, discover the Strait of Anian, open a land route to the Pacific, and take a look at the country northeastward beyond Quivira.

Sixty men went to the plains to procure meat and tallow and to capture buffalo to domesticate. After a few tilts the plan to tame the ugly beasts was given up, but more than two thousand pounds of tallow were obtained. Oñate went to Moqui, and from there Marcos Farfán led a party to the gold-fields of Arizona which Espejo had discovered, and staked out claims. On their way to join Oñate, Juan de Zaldívar and fourteen companions were slain at Ácoma, by the rebellious People of the White Rock. To punish the offenders Oñate sent out an expedition which captured Ácoma after two days of terrific fighting on its stone stairs, laid the pueblo waste by fire, and exterminated most of its inhabitants. Shortly afterward Oñate led eighty men down the Canadian River, crossed Oklahoma, and entered Quivira at Wichita, Kansas; but he was forced to retreat by

Indian hostility. Another golden dream had a prosaic awakening.

Meanwhile disaster had befallen the colony, which by this time had moved its headquarters across the Río Grande to San Gabriel, near Chama River. A dry season had made food scarce and, when Oñate returned, he confiscated the supplies in the pueblos, leaving the Indians destitute. The friars, whose first thought was for their missions, were now in conflict with Oñate. One of them wrote of him: "In all the expeditions he has butchered many Indians, human blood has been shed, and he has committed thefts, sackings, and other atrocities. I pray that God may grant him the grace to do penance for all his deeds." Hunger drove most of the settlers and all the friars but one back to Santa Bárbara. Among those who withdrew, ruined in fortune, was Captain Luís de Velasco, the erstwhile Beau Brummel of the satin coats. Oñate sent soldiers after his faint-hearted colonists to arrest and bring them back. Some of them returned, and Father Escobar came north as the new superior of the missionaries, bringing six new friars.

Finally, in 1604, Oñate carried out his intention of reaching the South Sea. It was his last throw of the dice. By this time he and his friends were ruined in fortune, and his reputation was under a cloud as a result of charges made by his rivals and enemies. New Mexico was already a white elephant on the royal hands. Oñate must make a hit somewhere, and Vizcaíno had just focused attention on California. Westward, therefore, Oñate again turned. With thirty men he followed the footsteps of Espejo and Farfán and went on to the Colorado, down the Colorado to the Gulf of California; explored the shore of the Gulf, found no pearl fisheries, and returned to San Gabriel convinced that California was an island. On the way he had heard from an Indian wag of a land to the north where people slept under water and wore golden bracelets; of a race of unipeds; of giant Amazons on a silver island to the west; of a tribe with long ears trailing on the ground, and of another nation which lived on smells. And, as Father Escobar indited of these matters, since God had created greater wonders and "since they have been affirmed by so many and different tribes . . . they cannot lack foundation."

New Mexico was an expense. It had not led to discovery of the Strait of Anian; the distant mines of Arizona could not be worked without Indian labor, which could only be procured by keeping a large and costly military force in the country. The new Viceroy of Mexico reported on the province unfavorably to the King and urged that all efforts now be concentrated on California. The colonists were as disheartened as the Viceroy. They threatened to leave if ample supplies did not arrive within the year. At the same time, in August, 1607, Oñate asked for his release, unless sufficient aid was to be sent to him. This may have been a bluff. If so, it was called. His request was granted and early in 1609 Pedro de Peralta arrived in San Gabriel as the new Governor with instructions to find a better site and move the capital and colony thither. Thus Peralta founded the town of Santa Fé. Oñate returned to Mexico, where the charges against him were pending for more than a decade. The rewards for his services were poverty, enemies, and disappointment. Nevertheless, he had founded a permanent outpost for Spain and a colony which after three centuries gives character to one of our commonwealths.

Hopes of finding rich minerals in New Mexico having failed, the province remained chiefly a missionary field, with its principal secular settlement at Santa Fé. But as a missionary province it flourished. According to Father Benavides, by 1630 there were fifty friars at work. Their twenty-five missions included ninety pueblos and sixty thousand converts. At each mission there were a school and workshops, where the neophytes were taught reading, writing, singing, instrumental music, and the manual arts.

The account which Father Benavides gives of the Queres missions is typical of all. "Passing forward another four leagues," he says, "the Queres nation commences with its first pueblo, that of San Felipe, and extends more than ten leagues in seven pueblos. There must be in them four thousand souls, all baptized. There are three monasteries with very costly and beautiful churches, aside from those which each pueblo has. These Indians are very dexterous in reading, writing, and playing on all kinds of instruments and are skilled in all the crafts, thanks to the great industry of the friars who converted them."

For eighty years Spaniards and Indians dwelt at peace with each other. But while the Indians accepted the religion of the friars, they also preserved their own — as they have preserved it to this day — and, under demands that they give it up, coupled with penances and punishments, they became sullen. Then, too, they were driven to labor for their conquerors. The secret bitterness flamed up in the Pueblo Revolt of 1680, led by Popé, a Tewa medicine man, who had suffered chains and flogging. At this time the Spanish population numbered nearly three thousand settlers, living chiefly in the upper Río Grande valley between Isleta and Taos. Besides the towns of Santa Fé and Santa Cruz de la Cañada, a settlement had also been formed on the river at El Paso, now the Mexican town of Juárez. In addition to the labor enforced on them, the Indians paid tribute yearly in cloth and maize for the benefit of the alien settlers. They were more than willing to listen to Popé when he talked of casting out the heavy-handed strangers. Popé — whipped out of San Juan for witchcraft — made his headquarters in Taos, whither he called the northern chiefs. The depth of his hatred for the Spaniards may be gauged by the fact that, having reason to suspect the fidelity of his son-in-law, Bua, governor of the San Juan pueblo, he slew him with his own hand. Isleta and the Piros pueblos to the south did not join in the conspiracy, but their lack was more than compensated by an alliance with the fierce Apaches. So masterly was Popé's generalship that the blow

fell simultaneously on all the settlements. **Men,**
women, children, and friars — over four hundred
all told — were slaughtered indiscriminately; the
churches, houses, and property destroyed. About
twenty-five hundred Spaniards escaped to the
settlement at El Paso.

For eighteen years the Indians held New Mexico. There was not a resident Spaniard north of
the El Paso district. In 1692 Governor Diego de
Vargas led an expedition for the reduction of the
province. The reclamation and fortification of
that territory, and the spread of Spanish rule
beyond it, had again become vital. Vargas reconquered New Mexico with comparatively little
bloodshed; for most of the pueblos, taken by surprise, submitted without a blow. But when Vargas returned in 1693 with a colony of eight hundred settlers, the northern towns made a stiff
resistance. It was not until the end of 1694 that
they were conquered. Taos, where the old conspiracy had had its roots, was sacked and burned.
The Indian warriors, taken prisoners in the battles,
were executed; hundreds of women and children
were made slaves. Once more in the following
year did the Indians rise to repel the invader, but
their strength was broken. A series of bloody

campaigns by Vargas and his successor, Cubero, crushed at last their heroic spirit. The reconquest was complete, and Spanish rule was made secure exactly a century after it had first been established by Oñate.

For another century and a quarter New Mexico continued under Spain; then it became a part of independent Mexico. It was a typical Spanish outpost, isolated and sluggish, quite unlike the lively mining and political centers of New Spain farther south. At Santa Fé a long succession of military governors ruled over the province and engaged sometimes in unsavory quarrels with the missionary superiors.

The Indian pueblos were missions under the spiritual control of the padres, and mimic municipalities with their own officers under the political and economic control of alcaldes, appointed by the Governor. In the larger pueblos Spanish and in the smaller half-caste alcaldes were usually appointed. The alcaldes appointed agents and seldom visited their Indian charges. The offices were means, not alone of controlling, but more particularly of exploiting the natives. Each pueblo was required to carry provisions to the alcalde's

home — a sheep a week, butter, beans, tortil-
las, and other provisions. The natives also rendered personal service on the alcalde's hacienda
or in his household. They planted, tilled, and
harvested his crops, sometimes going long distances and carrying their tools. When the wool or
the cotton was gathered it was parceled out to
the Indians to manufacture into fabrics — for the
alcalde's benefit. Women were required for household service, with resulting scandals. Indians
often bought, at high prices, freedom for their
women from this household service. The alcaldes
and the Governor monopolized most of the trade
with their pueblos   Weekly labor for the Governor was so distributed that Indians from Río
Arriba went to Santa Fé to work between Resur-
rection Day and All Saint's Day; those from Río
Abajo going during the rest of the year. Every
week five women were sent to grind corn and
do other work at the Governor's palace, while a
certain number of men worked on his haciendas.

For a picture of New Mexico in 1744 we are
indebted to Father Menchero, procurator of the
missions. The province included not only the settlements of the upper Río Grande but the El
Paso district as well, on both sides of the river.

At that time there were seven hundred and seventy-one households, or about ten thousand persons, for families were surprisingly large. Two-thirds of these people lived in the four principal cities of Santa Fé, Santa Cruz, Albuquerque, and El Paso. Of these El Paso was the largest. The remainder lived on haciendas and ranchos — rural villages they were, ranging from five to forty-six families each. The Franciscans still administered twenty-five missions, each containing from thirty to one hundred families. Nineteen of these missions were in the upper district, between Isleta and Taos, Pecos and Zuñi. Six were strung along the Río Grande below El Paso within a distance of twenty leagues. All these were then on the right bank of the stream, but subsequent changes in the river bed have left some of them in Texas. Population increased slowly but steadily to the end of Spanish rule, when the province, not counting the El Paso district, had thirty thousand settlers.

The Spaniards, so-called, were by no means all full-blood Castilians. In every frontier Spanish colony the soldiery was to a large extent made up of castes — mestizos, coyotes, and mulattoes — and New Mexico was no exception to the rule. As time went on, the Indian admixture increased. The laws of the Indies provided that Spaniards and castes should not settle in the Indian towns and missions, on the theory that the association was bad for the Indian. Nevertheless, before the end of the eighteenth century many Spaniards, and especially the castes, settled in the Indian pueblos, where they gained possession of the Indian lands, and by getting the Indians in their debt, kept them in practical peonage. Similarly, the castes often got control of the pueblo government. The Indians were required by law to nominate their own "governors," but in many cases the coyotes and mulattoes managed to secure the election.

Of all the elements in the population none was more unhappy than the *genizaros*, or Janissaries. These were Indians of various tribes of the plains, ransomed or captured in childhood, employed as servants, and Christianized. They were employed especially as scouts and as auxiliaries in campaigns, hence their name. They were an extraneous element in society, and they tended to segregate themselves from both Spaniards and Pueblos. Frequently they ran away. For these outcasts the missionaries in 1740 founded a mission settlement at Thomé on the Río Grande, just below Isleta; others were founded later at Belén and Sabinal.

The river valleys of New Mexico were highly productive. Irrigation was commonly practiced. In the upper districts maize, wheat, cotton, garden truck, cattle, sheep, goats, horses, mules, and fowls were raised on a considerable scale. Sheep raising flourished especially in the north, and cattle abounded at Taos and Soledad. The Indians manufactured fabrics of cotton, wool, buffalo, deer, and rabbit hides. At Albuquerque woolen and cotton fabrics were woven by the Spaniards. At El Paso a fine *acequia* watered large fields of wheat and maize and vineyards which produced "fine wine in no way inferior to that of Spain." Some of the haciendas were large and productive. That of Captain Rubín de Celis, ten leagues below El Paso, had on it twenty Spanish families. The Treval hacienda, at Laguna, customarily planted two hundred fanegas (400 bushels) of wheat and three hundred fanegas of maize, all by means of tributary Indian labor.

At Taos annual fairs were held. Wild Indians brought captive children and buffalo and deer skins, to exchange for horses, mules, knives,

hatchets, and trinkets.   The Moqui pueblos had
a large commerce in cattle and fabrics with the
surrounding tribes, particularly with the Yumas
and Mojaves of the Colorado River.   The Spaniards conducted Indian trade at long distances,
making frequent or even annual expeditions to the
Jumanos of central Texas, to the Pawnees and the
Arapahoes beyond the Arkansas, and to the various tribes of the Utah Basin, as far as Lake Utah.
The monopolistic system of Spain restricted external
trade to narrow channels.   The great commercial
event of the year was the departure of the annual
caravan of cattle, carts, and pack mules, bound for
Chihuahua, whither exports were sent and whence
manufactured articles were obtained.

In the eighteenth century the French of Louisiana began to smuggle into New Mexico much
needed merchandise.   After Louisiana passed into
the hands of Spain, communication was opened
with St. Louis, and trade with the Plains Indians
increased.   Early in the nineteenth century American traders and adventurers attempted to enter
the country, but usually fell into Spanish prisons.
In 1806 Zebulon Pike, the American explorer, was
captured by Spaniards and taken to Santa Fé.   To
his American eye Santa Fé's one-story houses of

thick adobe walls looked from a distance "like a fleet of flat-boats which are seen in the spring and fall seasons descending the Ohio. . . . The public square is in the center of the town, on the north side of which is situated the palace or government house, with the quarters for the guards, etc. The other side of the square is occupied by the clergy and public officers. . . . The streets are very narrow, say, in general, twenty-five feet. The supposed population is 4500."

When Mexico threw off the Spanish yoke in 1821, New Mexico became a province of Mexico, with a northern boundary at the forty-second parallel, including Colorado, Utah, Nevada, and most of Arizona. The exclusive policy of Spain was now relaxed, and American trappers and traders found free access. American pioneers like Kit Carson and Charles Bent adopted the country and married its daughters; and traders opened the great caravan trade from St. Louis to Santa Fé, thence to Chihuahua and to Los Angeles. When New Mexico passed into American hands the population had reached sixty thousand — a figure about equal to the total French population in North America at the end of the French régime.

CHAPTER VII

On the Pacific slope the frontiers of effective settlement marched northward by slow degrees into Arizona and Lower California. This advance was led throughout the seventeenth century by Spanish Jesuits, contemporaries of the better known Black Robes in Canada. Laboring in a much more propitious field, they were able to achieve more permanent results than their less numerous and less fortunate French brothers in the Canadian wilderness. The Jesuits on the Pacific slope made important contributions to civilization. A large part of the population in this area today has sprung from ancestors, on one side or the other, who got their first touch of European culture in the Jesuit missions and most of the towns and cities of today have grown up on the sites of early missions.

Missions were an integral part of Spain's scheme

of conquest.   Experience on the frontiers of Mexico, repeated in Florida, proved that the methods
of such conquerors and pacificators as Guzmán and
De Soto had worked ill on the whole.   A mass of
legislation and royal instructions issued in the
seventeenth century indicates that the authorities
desired to approximate to that ideal of conquest
through love for which Fray Luís Cancer had, long
ago, laid down his life on the sands of Florida.

The Indians had a definite place in the Spanish
scheme.   Apart from the fact that Indian wars
were costly, Spain wished to have the natives
preserved and rendered docile and contented wards
of the government.   She needed their toil, because
of the dearth of Spanish laborers.   Furthermore
she lacked white settlers.   She planned, therefore, to gather the Indians into permanent villages,
to civilize them, and to use them as a bulwark
against other European powers who might seek to
plant colonies on her territory.   Not to the conquistador could she look for fulfillment of this
design.   For, though his contract bade him be
tender, it offered him no means of enriching himself
except through the fortuitous discovery of precious
metals or pearls — or by plundering and exploiting the natives.   Spain turned to the missionaries

because the Indians were "well disposed to receive
the friars" — as Mendoza had written to the King
in describing Guzmán's devastations in Sinaloa —
"while they flee from us as stags fly in the forest."[1]

In the early days of conquest in the West Indies
and Mexico the control of the Indians had been
largely in the hands of trustees, called *encomen-
deros*.   They were secular persons, for the most
part, entrusted (*encomendar* means to entrust)
with the conversion, protection, and civilization
of the natives, in return for the right to exploit
them.   In theory the scheme was benevolent.   But
human nature is weak, and the tendency of the
trustee was to give his attention chiefly to exploitation and to neglect his obligations.   As a result
the *encomienda* became a black spot in the Spanish colonial system.   Efforts were made to abolish
the evil, and by slow degrees some progress was
achieved.   Then, too, as the frontiers expanded,
the institution tended to die a natural death.
Civilized Aztecs were worth the trouble of conquering; wild Apaches and warlike Creeks hardly, for
the cost of subduing them was disproportionate to
the returns from their labor.

On the new frontiers, therefore, the care and

[1] Lowery, *Spanish Settlements*, vol. i. p. 400.

control of the Indians was given over largely to the missionaries, aided by soldiers.   The missionaries were expected to convert, civilize, and control the Indians, without the old abuses of exploitation. So it was that in the seventeenth and eighteenth centuries missions became almost universal on the frontiers.   They operated simultaneously in the still unsubdued areas of northern Mexico, and in South Carolina, Georgia, Florida, Texas, New Mexico, Arizona, and Lower California.

It was in 1591 that the Jesuits, having after vain labors abandoned the Atlantic coast, first entered Sinaloa to heal the wounds made by the conquerors, and to gather together, convert, and civilize the remains of the native population.   As they went slowly northward, tribe by tribe, valley by valley, they founded missions beside the streams, attracted the natives to them by gifts and the display of religious pictures and images, baptized them, and gradually influenced them to collect in villages about the missions, to submit to the discipline of the padre in charge, to cultivate the soil, and to learn a few simple arts and crafts. By the middle of the seventeenth century they had reached the upper Sonora valley.   Meanwhile settlers had crept in behind the missionaries to engage in mining, grazing, and agriculture. These little outposts on the Pacific coast mainland became a base for later developments in adjacent California.

The man who led the way into Arizona and Lower California was one of the heroic figures of American history — Eusebio Francisco Kino. This hardy Jesuit was born near Trent in 1645, of Italian parentage, and was educated in Austria. He distinguished himself as a student at Freiburg and Ingolstadt and, in consequence, was offered a professorship in mathematics at the royal university of Bavaria. He rejected the offer and vowed himself to the missionary service, as a follower of Saint Francis Xavier, to whose intercession he attributed his recovery from a serious illness. He had hoped to go to the Far East, literally to follow in the footsteps of his patron, but there came a call for missionaries in New Spain and hither he came instead. Arriving in 1681, he proceeded two years later, as rector of missions, with an expedition designed to colonize the peninsula of California. The natives, though among the lowest in intelligence and morality of any tribes in America, were unwarlike and tractable on the whole. But a prolonged drought on the mainland, the base for supplies, caused the abandonment of the enterprise.

Destiny reserved for Kino a more promising field. Missions had already been established over all of southern and eastern Sonora. But beyond, to the west and north, lay the virgin territory of Pimería Alta, home of the upper Pimas, a region which comprised what is now northern Sonora and southern Arizona. At that day it was all included in the district of Sonora, to which it belonged until 1853, when the northern portion was cut off by the Gadsden Purchase.

Father Kino arrived in Pimería Alta in March, 1687, the very month when La Salle met his death in the wilds of central Texas, and began a term of service that was to last for twenty-four years. The frontier mission station when he arrived was at Cucurpe, in the valley of the river now called San Miguel. Cucurpe still exists, a quiet little Mexican pueblo, sleeping under the shadow of the mountains, and inhabited by descendants of Indians who were there in Kino's time.

Some fifteen miles above Cucurpe, on the San Miguel River, Kino founded the mission of Neustra Señora de los Dolores — Our Lady of Sorrows. The site chosen was one of peculiar fitness and beauty. Nearby the little San Miguel breaks through a narrow canyon, whose walls rise several hundred feet in height. Above and below the gorge the river valley broadens out into rich *vegas*, or irrigable bottom lands, half a mile or more in width and several miles in length. On the east the valley is walled in by Sierra de Santa Teresa, on the west by the Sierra del Torreón. Closing the lower valley and hiding Cucurpe stands Cerro Prieto; and cutting off the observer's view toward the north rises the grand and rugged Sierra Azul. At the canyon where the river breaks through, the western mesa juts out and forms a cliff approachable only from the east. On this promontory, protected on three sides from attack, and affording a magnificent view, was placed the mission of Dolores. Here still stand its ruins, in full view of the valley above and below, of the mountain walls on the east and west, the north and south, and within the sound of the rushing cataract of the San Miguel as it courses through the gorge. This meager ruin on the cliff, consisting now of a mere fragment of an adobe wall and saddening piles of débris, is the most venerable of all the many mission remains in Arizona and northern Sonora, for Our Lady of Sorrows was mother of them all, and for nearly a quarter of a century was the home of the remarkable missionary who built them.

From his station at Dolores, Kino and his companions, Jesuits and soldiers, pushed the frontier of missionary work and exploration across Arizona to the Gila and Colorado rivers. Most faithful amongst his associates, and his companion on many a long journey over the deserts, was Lieutenant Juan Mange, who, like Kino, has left us excellent accounts of these pioneer days.

Kino began his exploration into what is now Arizona in 1691. He was accompanied on his first journey by Father Salvatierra, who had come from the south as a visitor. They went north as far as Tumacácori, a Pima village on the Santa Cruz River, now the site of a venerable mission ruin. In the following year Kino reached San Xavier del Bac and entered the valley of the San Pedro, north of Douglas. At Bac he spoke to the natives the word of God, "and on a map of the world showed them the lands, the rivers, and the seas over which we fathers had come from afar to bring them the saving knowledge of the holy faith"; so giving them a lesson in geography, as well as a bit of Gospel truth. Two years later Kino descended the Santa Cruz River to the Casa Grande, the famous ruin on the Gila River, of which in his writings he gives us the first description. "The *casa grande*," he observes, "is a four-story building, as large as a castle, and equal to the largest church in these lands of Sonora. It is said that the ancestors of Montezuma deserted and depopulated it, and, beset by the neighboring Apaches, left for the East, or Casas Grandes, [1] and that from there they turned toward the south and southwest, finally founding the great city of Mexico." Mange adds a note of description. He mentions the thick walls of "strong cement and clay . . . so smooth on the inside that they resemble planed boards, and so polished that they shine like Puebla pottery."

Despite his success amongst the Pimas, Father Kino had never lost interest in the Indians of Lower California, and in 1695 he and Salvatierra, still working in unison, went to Mexico to urge a new attempt to found missions there. Two years later the two had the distinction — always cherished by Kino — of being personally named by the King to head the work. But the settlers in Sonora clamored to have Kino remain in Pimería Alta, where he was needed to help keep the Indians quiet, and Father Picolo went with Salvatierra instead. But on Kino's continued support the success of the work largely depended.

[1] In Chihuahua.

The difficulty of sending supplies across the **Gulf** to Salvatierra's new missions quickened Kino's interest in northwestern exploration, and brought about a revolution in his geographical notions. He had come to America with the belief that California was a peninsula, but, under the influence of current teachings, he had accepted the theory that it was an island. During his journey to the Gila in 1699, however, the Indians had made him a present of some blue shells, such as he had seen on the western coast of California and nowhere else. He now reasoned that, as the Indians could not have crossed the Gulf, California must be, after all, a peninsula, and that it might be possible to find a land route over which to send provisions and stock to Salvatierra's struggling establishments. To test this theory was the principal object of Kino's later explorations. By 1702 he had explored the Colorado from the mouth of the Gila to the Gulf and had proved, to his own satisfaction at least, that Lower California was not an island but a peninsula. The map which he made of his explorations, published in 1705, was not improved upon for more than a century.

As Kino explored and questioned natives about blue shells and hidden trails over the arid deserts and the stark peaks, he baptized and taught in little huts which the wondering Indians built to serve as chapels. Kino's diaries reveal not only a consuming zeal for his faith, but a deep love and paternal care for his red-skinned flock. He was not satisfied with itinerant preaching, which left the Indians to revert to their pagan ways between his visits; but he gathered them into missions as the law required. By 1696 Kino had begun to prepare for resident missions in Arizona by founding stock ranches in the Santa Cruz and San Pedro valleys, and four years later had begun the building of San Xavier del Bac, near the present Tucson, which is in use to this day. On April 28, 1700, he wrote in his diary: " . . . we began the foundations of a very large and capacious church and house of San Xavier del Bac, all the many people working with much pleasure and zeal, some in digging for the foundations, others in hauling many and very good stones of *tezontle*, [1] from a little hill which was about a quarter of a league away. For the mortar for these foundations it was not necessary to haul water, because by means of the irrigation ditches we very easily conducted the water where we wished. And that house, with its great court and

[1] A porous stone much used by Mexicans for building.

garden nearby, will be able to have throughout the year all the water it may need, running to any place or work-room one may please, and one of the greatest and best fields in all Nueva Biscaya."[1]

The "many people" were three thousand Indians who had gathered to meet him and to beseech him to remain with them. Kino was willing, for he regarded San Xavier as the strategic point in his plans for advance. He asked permission to move his headquarters thither, but he was needed elsewhere, and in his stead Father Gonzalvo was sent. In the same year Mission San Gabriel was built at Guebavi and Father San Martín was installed there. For the support of his missions and the Indians who gathered about them Kino started large stock and grain farms; and once at least he sent as many as seven hundred head of cattle to his brethren on the Peninsula of California.

As an explorer Kino ranks among the greatest of the Southwest. From Mission Dolores, during the twenty-four years of his ministry, he made over fifty journeys, which varied in length from a hundred to a thousand miles. He crossed repeatedly in various directions all the country between the Magdalena and the Gila rivers and between the

[1] Bolton, *Kino's Historical Memoir*, vol. II, pp. 235–36.

San Pedro and the Colorado. One of his trails lay over the waterless Devil's Highway, where scores of adventurers have since lost their lives. Sometimes his only companions were a few Indian servants. But he usually traveled with plenty of horses and mules from his ranches, sometimes as many as a hundred and thirty head. His physical hardihood was great, and there are many stories of his hard riding. More than once, like a general, Kino mustered his Pima children and sent them out to war against the unsociable Apaches. And, when the Spanish authorities disputed the number of Apache scalps they were requested to pay for, it was Kino who galloped off to count the scalps and see to it that his children were not stinted of their bonus. For himself, he cherished hardship. He ate sparingly, drank no wine, and went meagerly clothed.

Kino's last days were to him a time of stagnation and disappointment. The Spanish monarchy was at its lowest ebb, and funds for the support of the missions were not to be had unless they served some important political purpose. Texas, not Arizona, was the danger point now, and funds had to be used there. Kino died in 1711 at Magdalena, one of the missions which he had founded, across

the mountains from Dolores. He was not yet
seventy. Father Velarde, a companion, has thus
described his last moments: "He died as he had
lived, with extreme humility and poverty. . . .
His deathbed, as his bed had always been, consisted of two calfskins for a mattress, two blankets
such as the Indians use for covers, and a pack-
saddle for a pillow. . . . No one ever saw in him
any vice whatsoever, for the discovery of lands and
the conversion of souls had purified him. . . .
He was merciful to others but cruel to himself."

For two decades now the Arizona frontier slum-
bered. Then, Apache depredations in Sonora, a
military inspection, and a visit by the Bishop of
Durango shook it to renewed life. A missionary
revival followed. In 1732 a new band of Jesuits,
mainly Germans — Keler, Sedelmayr, Steiger,
Grashofer, Paver — took up the work which the
great founder had laid down with his life. San
Xavier and others of the abandoned missions were
reoccupied. Interest in the border was enhanced
by a mining "rush" in 1736. Immense nuggets of
free silver were found at Arizonac, in the upper Altar valley, just over the present Sonora line. It is
from this place that the State of Arizona gets its
name. For a time the region fairly hummed with

life, but after five years the mines played out and there was another dozing spell. A Pima uprising in 1751 caused another awakening. To hold the district a presidio was built at Tubac in 1752. Here the military frontier halted for twenty-four years, and then it advanced to Tucson.

Meanwhile Salvatierra and his companions — for others had joined him from time to time — were succeeding across the Gulf of California. Having slender royal aid, the missionaries had to depend at first on private alms. In a short time prominent individuals had contributed $47,000, which constituted the nucleus of the famous Pious Fund of California. Missionary beginnings were made at Loreto, halfway up the inner coast of the Peninsula. Soon a palisaded fort and church were constructed there, and within a year Salvatierra had four launches plying back and forth, to and from the mainland. Gradually the work extended to the surrounding country, new missions were founded in the neighborhood, and explorations were made across the Peninsula to the Pacific. Salvatierra was much interested in Kino's efforts to establish a land route between Arizona and Lower California, and joined him, in 1701, on one of his expeditions

In a report written in February, 1702, Father Picolo, in fervid and poetic language tells of the landing of himself and Salvatierra and depicts their mission as it appeared to them in their spirit of exaltation and sacrifice. They had taken, he wrote, "as the guiding star of our voyage that star of the sea, the most devoted image of the Lady of Loreto, which led us without mishap to the desired port." And on landing they had set up the image "as decently as the country and our poverty would permit" and had placed the "undertaking in her hands" that she, like a "beneficent sun," might banish the pagan night blinding the Indians with the shadows of death. Satan had not watched the coming of the padres unmoved at the prospect of losing "his ancient and peaceful possession" of heathen souls.

As he blinded their understandings, they could not comprehend the words of the light which, with resplendent rays, spoke the language of heaven for their welfare, while we, upon hearing a language which we had not known, could not in ours, which they had not heard, make known to them the high purpose, for them so advantageous, which had taken us to their lands. And although we had gone to their shores solely to seek the precious pearls of their souls, to nurture them with the heavenly dew of the Divine Word, and to give them their luster in Christ, showing them the celestial shell Mary, who conceived for their good, with the gentle dew of heaven, the perfect pearl of first luster, Christ, they thought we came like others who at other times, sometimes not without injury to their people, had landed on their shores in search of the many and rich pearls which were produced in the countless fisheries of their coast. With this opinion quickened at the instigation of the Devil, . . . they attacked our little guard . . . with such fury and so thick a shower of arrows and stones that if the Lady had not constituted an army to resist it . . . our purpose would have been frustrated. With this glorious triumph their pride was humbled. . . . Some of them came to our camp. . . . Then through easy intercourse with them we devoted all our efforts to learning their language.[1]

Salvatierra followed the same plan which Kino and his associates employed in establishing their work. He sent a padre, or went himself, to visit a tribe, to make gifts and to talk of religion, until the Indians were won over and were willing to have a mission erected in their village. Each new mission was placed within easy communication of one already established from which supplies could be drawn until the new mission was able to support itself. Some fifteen missions were ultimately established in Salvatierra's domain by separate

[1] Bolton, *Kino's Historical Memoir*, vol. II, pp. 47–49.

endowment made through the charity and zeal of some rich Catholic who sought by this means his own grace and the benefit of the heathen. Two were endowed with ten thousand pesos each by a "priest commissioner of the court of the Holy Office of the Inquisition," another by certain members of a Jesuit college in Mexico; but the greater part of the Pious Fund was contributed by non-clericals. Patiently Salvatierra and his assistants went on their chosen task, erecting missions, gathering the Indians in pueblos under trustworthy native alcaldes, teaching them agriculture, stock raising, saddlery, and shoemaking, improving on the native fashion of weaving, and — for the beautifying of the church services and for their own innocent entertainment — instructing them in music and singing.

In the midst of his work Salvatierra was called to Mexico to serve as provincial of New Spain, but at the expiration of his term he returned and continued his work till 1717. For twenty years the history of Lower California had been little more than his own biography. After Salvatierra's death more liberal aid was provided, and new missions were established both in the south and the north. Before their expulsion the Jesuits had founded missions and opened trails throughout almost the entire length of the peninsula.

The lives of such men as Kino and Salvatierra — and of some of their associates who met martyrdom at the hands of their flocks — are the undimming gold of one side of the shield. It was for what he professed to see on the reverse side of that shield that Carlos III, in 1767, banished the Jesuits from his dominions. For a year or two the Franciscans occupied the former Jesuit field; but, when a new advance north was made, the Peninsula was assigned to the Dominicans and Alta California to the Franciscans.

The work of the Jesuits in Lower California had opened the way for the colonization of Alta California. The preparations for settlement were made at Loreto and other mission towns, from which the land expeditions started; and the ships from Mexico were overhauled and stocked in seaports on the Peninsula. Thus the first stages of the northward journey of the founders of California were made through a province where peaceable natives and a chain of missions and mission farms reduced the hazards of the march.

CHAPTER VIII

TEXAS

In the sixteenth century Spain, as we have seen, had thrust up into the North the two outposts of Florida and New Mexico. In time foreign intrusion made it necessary to occupy the intervening region called Texas, which embraced a goodly slice of what is now Louisiana. While Spain was busy farther south, other nations were encroaching on her northern claims. By 1670 England had planted strong centers of colonization all the way from Jamaica to New England, and had erected trading posts on Hudson Bay. French traders from Canada, meanwhile, had been pushing up the St. Lawrence to the Great Lakes and branching north and south through the wilderness. At the same time French and English buccaneers from the West Indies were marauding the Florida settlements and the coast towns of Mexico. English, French, and Spanish territorial claims and frontier settlements clashed. The lines of competition, imperial and commercial, were drawing tighter with every passing year.

On the Atlantic coast the Anglo-Spanish frontiers clashed with resounding echo from the very moment of the founding of Charleston (1670), just across from the Spanish outpost Santa Elena, on Port Royal Sound. If Plymouth Rock and Hudson Bay were too remote to have a direct influence on Spanish claims, nevertheless their indirect influence — through the acceleration they gave to French activities — was to be potent. France's opportunity, indeed, seemed golden. And it was in the West. In Europe France was rapidly taking the position of supremacy which had been Spain's; and New France promised to become not only a valuable source of revenue through the fur trade — if the wide beaver lands "beyond" could be secured — but also the point of control over the Strait of Anian for which French explorers as well as Spanish sought. The French had heard also of a great river flowing through the continent; they hoped to discover that river and thus control the best trade route to China. When Joliet and Marquette descended the Mississippi to the Arkansas in 1673 and returned to publish their news in Quebec, some of their hearers at least believed that the river had been found.

Chief of these was Robert Cavelier de la Salle, a recent arrival in Canada. La Salle hurried to France and laid before the King a plan to extend the fur trade to the Illinois country and explore the Mississippi, which rose in Asia, to its mouth. Four years later, having erected posts in Illinois, La Salle landed at the mouth of the Mississippi and claimed the territory along its course for France. The discovery that the river emptied into the Mexican Gulf put a new idea into La Salle's fertile brain. He made another journey to France and proposed to plant a colony at the mouth of the Mississippi, and thus to secure the river highway for France and establish a vantage point for the control of the Gulf and for descent upon the Spanish mines of northern Mexico. In the summer of 1684 he sailed from France with his colony; and toward the end of the year he landed on the Texas coast at Matagorda Bay. It was because of faulty maps, perhaps, that he had missed the mouth of the Mississippi. One of his four ships had been captured by Spaniards *en route* and another was wrecked on entering the bay. Beaujeu, the naval commander, who had quarreled with La Salle from the first, turned his vessel about and returned to France, carrying away some of the soldiers and a large quantity of much needed supplies. Tonty, La Salle's lieutenant in the Illinois country, who was to meet him at the mouth of the Mississippi with men and provisions, found no trace of him there and, after vain waiting, returned to the Illinois post.

Indian attacks and an epidemic worked havoc among the settlers, and La Salle moved his colony to a better site on the Garcitas River near the head of Lavaca Bay.[1] He set out from this point in search of the Mississippi, which he believed to be near, expecting to meet with Tonty. While he was exploring the eastern waters of Matagorda Bay, the last of his ships was wrecked. La Salle then started overland, northeastward. He reached the Nasoni towns north of the present Nacogdoches in northeastern Texas, some eighty miles from the Red River. Illness, and the desertion of some of his men, forced him to retrace his steps. He found his colony, a mere handful now, facing starvation. Though worn with hardships and fatigue, La Salle resolved on the effort to bring help from the

[1] Not on the Lavaca River as stated by Parkman and Winsor. The author in 1914 determined that the site of the colony was five miles above the mouth of the Garcitas River on the ranch of Mr. Claude Keeran, in Victoria County, Texas.

Illinois posts. This would seem a hopeless undertaking; for he had not found the Mississippi, by
which he had previously descended from the Illinois
country, and he had no idea of the distances he
must travel across an unknown wilderness. He
set out nevertheless with a few companions, including his brother, the Abbé Jean Cavelier, and his
nephew Moranget. He crossed the Colorado near
the present Columbus and, keeping on northward,
forded the Brazos just above Navasota. Here he
was treacherously slain by some of his men,[1] who
had already killed Moranget.

The survivors of La Salle's party continued
northeastward. Some deserted in the Indian towns.
The others, including La Salle's brother, crossed
the Red River near Texarkana and the intervening
country to the mouth of the Arkansas, ascended
to Tonty's post on the Illinois, and returned to
Canada. They did not inform Tonty of La Salle's
death, nor of the perilous condition of the little colony on the Gulf. Except for two or three men and
some children, who were taken by the Indians —
nine persons in all — the whole colony perished.

[1] Historians have supposed that this dastardly act was committed near the Trinity or the Neches, but evidence now avail-
able makes it clear that the spot was between the Brazos and
Navasota rivers and near the present city of Navasota.

When the mishaps attending La Salle's venture are reviewed — including a former attempt to poison him, the capture of one of his ships by the Spaniards, the desertion of Beaujeu, his assassination and the suppression of the news of it from the faithful Tonty who might have succored the colony — it is difficult not to suspect that his efforts were beset with subtle treachery from the beginning.

If the news of La Salle's expedition caused a sensation in Spain, it roused the greatest alarm along the whole northern Spanish frontier in the New World, from Chihuahua to Cuba. The West Indies were no longer solely Spanish. The progress of the century had brought English, French, and Dutch to the lesser islands neglected by Spain. English settlers now occupied the Bermudas and several other islands. English arms had taken Jamaica and, in the peace concluded in 1670, Spain had recognized England's right to it and to the others she had colonized. The French West India Company had founded colonies on Guadeloupe, Martinique, and in the Windward Islands. The Dutch had trading stations on St. Eustatius, Tobago, and Curaçao; and English, French, and Dutch held posts in Guiana. Raids from these bases on Spanish ports and treasure fleets were all

too frequent and too costly, even if nc recent buc-
caneer had rivaled the exploit of Piet Heyn of the
Dutch West India Company who, in 1628, had
chased the Vera Cruz fleet into Matanzas River,
Cuba, and captured its cargo worth $15,000,000.

That sons of a France growing swiftly in power
had pushed south from Canada through the hinter-
land and planted themselves on the Gulf where
they could coöperate with the lively pirates of the
French Indies was news to stir Mexico, Florida,
and the Spanish West Indies to a ferment. The
Spanish authorities hastily sent out expeditions
east and west by sea and land to discover and de-
molish La Salle's colony. Mariners from Vera Cruz
returned to that harbor to report two wrecked
French ships in Matagorda Bay and no sign of
a colony. It was concluded that La Salle's expedition had been destroyed and that the French
menace was over, for the time being at least.

The outposts in New León and Coahuila, just
south of the Río Grande, had been no less roused
than the harbor towns of Havana and Vera Cruz.
To the Spanish frontiersmen, dreaming even yet
of a rich kingdom "beyond," the thought of a
French colony expanding to bar their way was intolerable. Their spirit was embodied in the figure

of Alonso de León. A frontiersman by birth and training, famed for a score of daring exploits as a border fighter, Alonso de León was well fitted for the task to which the needs of the time summoned him. Under orders from Mexico, in 1686, León set off from Monterey on the first of his expeditions in search of La Salle's colony, following the south bank of Río Grande to the Gulf of Mexico. Next year he reconnoitered the north bank. But not till his third expedition did he come in direct touch with the French peril. He was now governor of Coahuila, at Monclova. This time he encountered a tribe of Indians north of the Río Grande who were being ruled with all a chief's pomp by a Frenchman called by the Spaniards Jarri. It appears that Jarri was not one of La Salle's settlers, but an independent adventurer who had wandered thus early into southwestern Texas from the Illinois country or from Canada. He was promptly stripped of his feathers, of course, and sent to Mexico to be questioned by the Viceroy.

The officials were now thoroughly frightened. A new expedition was immediately sent out under León, who took with him Father Damián Massanet, a Franciscan friar, the Frenchman Jarri, one hundred soldiers, and seven hundred mules and

horses. León could at least promise the Indians
a show of Spanish pomp and power. In March,
1689, León crossed the Río Grande and, bearing
eastward, crossed the Nueces, Frío, San Antonio,
and Guadalupe rivers. Late in April he came upon
the site of La Salle's settlement. There stood five
huts about a small wooden fort built of ship plank-
ing, with the date "1684" carved over the door.
The ground was scattered with weapons, casks,
broken furniture, and corpses. Among some Indians a few leagues away León found two of the
colonists, one of whom had had a hand in La Salle's
murder. He learned also that Tonty had erected
a fort on a river inland, the Arkansas, or perhaps
the Illinois. On the Colorado River León and Massanet had a conference with the chief of the Nabedache tribe, who had come from the Neches River
to meet them. The chief promised to welcome
missionaries at his village.

León returned to make a report in which piety and business sense are eloquently combined.
"Certainly it is a pity," he admonished, "that
people so rational, who plant crops and know that
there is a God, should have no one to teach them
the Gospel, especially when the province of Texas
is so large and fertile and has so fine a climate."

A large and fertile country already menaced by the French did indeed call for missions. León was dispatched a fifth time with one hundred and ten soldiers to escort Massanet and his chosen helpers to the Nabedache towns of the Asinai (Texas) Indians, near the Neches River in eastern Texas. On the way they paused long enough for Father Massanet to set fire to La Salle's fort. As the Spaniards were approaching their objective from the Southwest, Tonty on a second journey to seek La Salle — in Illinois he had heard sinister reports through the Indians — reached the Red River and sent an Indian courier to the Nabedache chief to request permission to make a settlement in his town. On being told of León's proximity Tonty retreated. The fleur-de-lis receded before the banner of Castile. The Spanish flag was raised at the Nabedache village in May, 1690, before the eyes of the wondering natives, formal possession was taken and the mission of San Francisco was founded. The expedition now turned homeward, leaving three Franciscan friars and three soldiers to hold Spain's first outpost in Texas.

Another expedition, after Alonso de León's death in 1691, set out from Monclova under Domingo Terán, a former governor of Sinaloa and

Senora, accompanied by Massanet to found more missions, on the Red River as well as the Neches. Terán returned without having accomplished anything, largely because of violent quarrels with Massanet, who opposed the planting of presidios beside the missions. Massanet remained with two friars and nine soldiers — the peppery padre protesting against the presence even of the nine. He soon learned that soldiers were sometimes needed. The Indians, roused by their leaders, turned against the missionaries and ordered them to depart. There was no force to resist the command. On October 25, 1693, Massanet applied the torch to the first Spanish mission in Texas, even as he had earlier fired La Salle's French fort, and fled. Four soldiers deserted to the Indians. One of them, José Urrutia, after leading a career as a great Indian chief, returned to civilization, and became commander at San Antonio, where his descendants still live and are prominent. The other five, with the three friars, after three months of weary and hungry marching, during forty days of which they were lost, at last entered Coahuila.

For the time being Texas was now abandoned by both contestants. But the French traders were only looking for a better opportunity and a more advantageous spot to continue the conflict, which, on their side, was directed against England as well as Spain. They had learned that English fur traders from South Carolina had already penetrated to the Creeks and to other tribes east of the Mississippi and they feared that England would seize the mouth of the river. The Spaniards also were disturbed by the English. They had been driven, in 1686, out of Port Royal and northern Georgia. Now they were alarmed by English fur-trading expeditions into Alabama and by the discovery that the Indians of Mobile Bay had moved north to trade with the English of Carolina. Thus, while France prepared to carry out La Salle's plan to colonize the Gulf coast, Spain with jealous eye watched the movements of both England and France. It was a three-cornered struggle.

In 1697 the King of France, Louis XIV, commissioned Pierre Le Moyne d'Iberville, fighting trader, hero of the fur raids on Hudson Bay, and the most dashing military figure in New France, to found, on the Mexican Gulf, a colony to be named Louisiana. To forestall the French an expedition was immediately dispatched from Vera Cruz to Pensacola Bay, where in November, 1698, the post of San Carlos was erected and garrisoned. The

move was none too soon. In January (1699)
Iberville's fleet stood off the harbor and demanded
admittance. The commander of San Carlos refused courteously but firmly. Iberville rewarded
him for his compliments with others from the same
mint, withdrew, sailed westward, and built a fort
at Biloxi.

But there were to be no battles, at present,
between Spaniards and French for Louisiana. The
fate of that territory was settled in Europe. The
Spanish King, Charles II, died. He left no son;
and, forced by the danger that a dismembering war
for the succession would follow on his death, he
bequeathed the crown to his grandnephew, the
Duke of Anjou, grandson of Louis XIV and
French in blood, sympathies, and education. The
new King, Philip V, harkened readily enough to his
French grandfather's suggestion that, in order to
protect Spain's Gulf possessions from England,
France must be allowed to colonize Louisiana.
The Spanish War Council objected, and Philip
let the matter drop, but the French settlement
was quietly moved from Biloxi to Mobile Bay,
nearer to the Spanish border. When in 1702
the War Council heard of it and protested, they
were rebuked by Philip. Thus Spain, dominated

by a Bourbon King, was forced to permit the occupation of Louisiana by France.

Iberville's brother, the Sieur de Bienville, a brilliant and vigorous commander, was appointed in 1701 Governor of Louisiana. Bienville concentrated his energies on alliances with the tribes east and west of the Mississippi to prevent them from trafficking with the English and to divert the southern fur trade to the French posts. Bienville was succeeded in 1713 by Cadillac, founder of Detroit, who served for three years, but Bienville continued to be the life of the colony. By 1716 the Mississippi, Mobile, and Red rivers had been explored by Bienville's men, sometimes led by himself. And French traders from Canada and the Illinois had explored the Missouri for several hundred miles and had built posts southward from the Illinois to the lower Ohio. In 1718 Bienville founded New Orleans. France's hold was thus fastened upon Louisiana, and Spain's colonies round the Gulf were split in two.

During the sixteen years of Bienville's activity, disturbing rumors had reached the Spanish border. To New Mexico came reports of Frenchmen trading with the Pawnees and of French voyageurs on the rivers to the northeast. Though

in various Spanish expeditions from Santa Fé
against Comanches and Apaches no French were
seen, yet the fear of their approach increased.
Similar rumors were heard on the Río Grande
border. One not slow to take advantage of this
general alarm was Father Hidalgo, a Franciscan
who had been with Massanet at his mission in
Texas. The intervening years had been spent by
Hidalgo chiefly in founding and conducting missions in Coahuila, a work which had led the way for
the secular powers and thus pushed the frontier
of mining and ranching to the south bank of the
Río Grande. With heart burning for the welfare
of his former ungrateful charges, he had made
many earnest appeals to be allowed to return to
Texas, but the superiors of his Order would not
sanction his plea.[1] Hidalgo, with genuine political shrewdness, then resolved to turn the French
menace to good account. If he could prove that
Spain's territory of Texas was in imminent danger,
he knew that missions would be founded without
delay. So he wrote a letter in 1711 to the French

[1] A myth has found currency in recent years to the effect that,
despite this opposition, Hidalgo returned to Texas, dwelt for a
time among the Asinais and there wrote his appeal to the French
priests. But his writings preserved in the College of Querétaro in
Mexico and examined by the author disprove the story.

priests of Louisiana, begging them to "pacify the tribes hostile to the Asinai nation, who were nearer to their settlements, thereby to give the greatest honor and glory to God." Just why pacification of the Louisiana tribes bordering on the Texas Indians would honor Heaven more than missionary labors in other parts of Louisiana he did not make clear, but it is plain enough that the first result of the pacification would be the establishment of French posts near or among the Asinai. This might or might not honor Heaven, but it would undoubtedly interest Spain.

Father Hidalgo sent an Indian servant with the letter to the Asinai country, where it was confided to a Louisiana Indian who happened to be there. Getting no reply, a year later he sent out another letter, addressed to the Governor of Louisiana. Neither missive appears to have reached its address; but in May, 1713, the first letter — after having been handed about among Indians for two years — came into Governor Cadillac's possession. It interested Cadillac very much, for he had recently been instructed by Antoine Crozat, to whom Louis XIV had granted a monopoly of all the Louisiana commerce, to attempt to open trade with Mexico despite the rigorous Spanish commercial regulations. Cadillac had already tried by way of Vera Cruz and failed. Better luck might follow an attempt to open an overland route to the Río Grande border, where Spanish smugglers could be trusted to do the rest, for the stupid commercial systems of European governments at the time made habitual smugglers of all frontier dwellers in America. At any rate Hidalgo's letter inspired the Governor to make the effort, just as Hidalgo had probably surmised it would.

Cadillac chose his cleverest agent. He sent Louis Juchereau de St. Denis, explorer, fur trader, and commander at Biloxi, with instructions to visit Hidalgo, who, so Cadillac inferred from the letter, was among the Asinai, and to build a post on the Red River within easy access of their territory. St. Denis established the post of Natchitoches, put in the winter trading, and by spring was seeking Hidalgo in Texas. There he learned that the friar was on the Coahuila border, so on June 1, 1714, with three French companions and twenty-five Indians he set out on foot for the Río Grande. Strangely enough, two of his companions were the Talon brothers, survivors of the ill-fated La Salle expedition who had been ransomed from the Indians by León and Terán. On the 18th of July St. Denis reached Hidalgo's mission of San Juan, forty miles below Eagle Pass. Hidalgo had gone to Querétaro, but the other missionaries and Captain Ramón at the post received St. Denis hospitably, and Ramón wrote to Hidalgo that, in view of the French danger, "it looks to me as though God would be pleased that your Reverence would succeed in your desires." This letter reveals Father Hidalgo's finesse. While Ramón entertained St. Denis and dispatched messengers to the authorities in Mexico City asking what he should do with him, St. Denis improved his time by winning the heart of Ramón's granddaughter, Manuela Sánchez, who later went with him to Natchitoches and there reigned ten years as the Grand Dame of the post, becoming godmother, as the baptismal records show, of most of the children of the place.

A new French menace had arisen. The Viceroy of Mexico hastily decided to found new missions in Texas and to protect them this time by strong garrisons. St. Denis, having by his marriage and his cleverness ingratiated himself with the Spaniards, was engaged at five hundred dollars to guide the Texas expedition, which was commanded by Captain Domingo Ramón, his wife's cousin. It looks more like a family affair than an international

row.   Meanwhile Hidalgo had given the Viceroy
a satisfactory explanation of his random mis-
sives and had received permission to go to Texas
with the expedition.   The colony crossed the Río
Grande in April, 1716.   It consisted of sixty-five
persons, including soldiers, nine friars, and six
women, a thousand head of cattle, sheep, and
goats, and the equipment for missions, farms,
and garrison.   At the head of the missionaries
went two of Spain's most distinguished men in
America, Father Espinosa, the well-known historian, and Father Margil, whose great services
in the American wilds will probably result in his
canonization by the Papal Court.   The Asinais
welcomed the Spaniards and helped them to erect
four missions and a garrison near the Neches and
Angelina rivers.   Shortly afterward a mission was
built at Los Adaes (now Robeline) Louisiana, within fifteen miles of St. Denis's post of Natchitoches.

The success of the French traders with the
powerful tribes, the coming of John Law's colonists
to Louisiana, and the need of a halfway base, inspired the Spanish authorities to send out another
colony, to occupy a site at the beautiful San Pedro
Springs, on the San Antonio River, which lay on
the direct route between the Neches River and the

settlement at San Juan, near Eagle Pass. Early in
1718 the new colony, numbering some sixty whites,
with friars and Indian neophytes, founded San Antonio a few months before New Orleans was born.
And Father Olivares began the San Antonio, or
Alamo, Mission, which was later to become famous
as the shrine of Texas liberty.

Spain had at last occupied eastern Texas, but her
hold was not long undisturbed. In the following
year France and Spain went to war over European questions, and the conflict was echoed in the
American wilderness, all the way from Pensacola
to Platte River. Pensacola was captured by the
French, recaptured by the Spaniards, and taken
again by Bienville. The French at Natchitoches
descended upon Texas and the garrison retreated
to San Antonio without striking a blow. A plan
for conquering Coahuila and New Mexico was
drawn up on paper in Louisiana, perhaps by St.
Denis. Eight hundred Frenchmen and a large
body of Indian allies were to march overland from
Natchitoches, while a flotilla sailed along the Texas
coast and ascended the Río Grande. It was La
Salle's old plan in a new guise. St. Denis was made
"commander of the River of Canes" (the Colorado), and two expeditions were sent in 1720 and

1721 to take possession of Matagorda Bay. Both of them failed.

In New Mexico the Governor had heard, before the war broke out, that the French were settling on Platte River and, on his recommendation, the Viceroy ordered that alliances be made with the tribes to the northeast, a colony planted at El Cuartelejo in Colorado, and a presidio established on the North Platte — that is, at some point in the present Nebraska or Wyoming. In August, 1720, an expedition from New Mexico penetrated to the North Platte but, not finding any signs of a French colony, turned back. On the South Platte, in Colorado, it was almost totally annihilated by Indians armed with French weapons. Apparently tribes from as far north as Wisconsin took part in this fray, a fact which indicates the scope and power of the early French trader's influence. The end of the war in Europe caused the Viceroy to abandon his plans for colonizing to the north of New Mexico. The treaty of peace restored Pensacola to Spain.

Meanwhile affairs had moved apace on the Texas border. The Marquis of Aguayo, then Governor of Coahuila, undertook the reconquest, mainly at his own expense. Before the end of 1720 he had raised eight companies of cavalry, comprising over five hundred men and five thousand horses. It was the largest military expedition to enter the northern interior since the days of De Soto. Leaving Monclova in November, Aguayo strengthened San Antonio, and sent a garrison to occupy Matagorda Bay. Peace had now been declared, and at the Neches River Aguayo was met by St. Denis, who, swimming his horse across the stream for a parley, informed Aguayo that the war was over and agreed to permit an unrestricted occupation of the abandoned posts. Proceeding east, Aguayo reëstablished the six abandoned missions and the presidio of Dolores, and added a presidio at Los Adaes, facing Natchitoches. The expedition had been a success, but the poor horses paid a terrible price for the bloodless victory. The return journey to San Antonio, through a storm of sleet, was so severe that of his five thousand beasts only fifty were left alive when he arrived in January, 1722.

Aguayo had fixed the hold of Spain on Texas. It was he who clinched the nails driven by León, Massanet, Hidalgo, and Ramón. There were now in Texas ten missions, four presidios, and four centers of settlement — Los Adaes, Nacogdoches, San Antonio, and La Bahía (Matagorda Bay). A governor was appointed and the capital of the province fixed at Los Adaes, now Robeline, Louisiana. Originally the name Texas had applied only to the country east of the Trinity River, but now the western boundary was fixed at the Medina River. It was to be moved half a century later to the Nueces. After much petty quarreling with the French of Louisiana, the little Arroyo Hondo was made the eastern boundary, and thus for a century old Texas included a large strip of the present State of Louisiana.[1]

For twenty years after the Aguayo expedition, the Frenchman St. Denis, or "Big Legs," as the natives fondly called him, ruled the border tribes with paternal sway from his post at Natchitoches on the Red River. The relations of French and Spaniards on this border were generally amicable. Intermarriages and a mutual love of gayety made friendship a pleasanter and more natural condition for the Latin neighbors than strife. Indeed, when in June, 1744, the long career of the redoubtable St. Denis came to a close, prominent among those assembled at Natchitoches to assist in the funeral honors were Governor Boneo and Father Vallejo,

[1] In 1819, long after French rivalry had passed, the Sabine River was made the boundary. It is an error to suppose that it was originally the boundary between New France and New Spain.

from Los Adaes, across the international boundary line. And yet, when, a few days later, Boneo reported the event to his Viceroy in Mexico, he did so in terms which meant, "St. Denis is dead, thank God; now we can breathe more easily."

Spain's hold upon Texas was secure against France, but many a battle was yet to be fought for the territory with the ferocious Apaches and Comanches, and the incursions of French traders into the Spanish settlements continued to be a source of friction. The jealous trade policy of Spain only increased the eagerness of these traders to enter New Mexico, where the Pueblo Indians and the colonists alike were promising customers, if Spanish officers could be bribed or outwitted. For a long time the way from Louisiana was blocked by Apaches and Comanches, who were at war with the Louisiana tribes, and the river highways were unsafe. Canadians, however, conspicuous among them being La Vérendrye and his sons, descended from the north through the Mandan towns on the Missouri, reaching the borders of Colorado, and two brothers named Mallet succeeded in piercing the Indian barrier, entered New Mexico, and returned safely to Louisiana. The town of Gracia Real below Albuquerque where they lodged was given the nickname of "Canada." Later on French traders in numbers invaded New Mexico, some of whom were seized and sent to Mexico or to Spain and thrown into prison. Spanish troops were sent to guard the approaches to Chihuahua below El Paso; fears were felt for even distant California; and to keep the New Orleans traders from the Texas coast tribes, a presidio and a mission were established on the Louisiana border at the mouth of the Trinity River, near Galveston Bay.

But the scene soon shifted. The Seven Years' War removed France from the American continent, left Louisiana in the hands of Spain, and brought Spain and England face to face along the Mississippi.

CHAPTER IX

LOUISIANA

THE year 1759 was a fateful one in North America, for it recorded the fall of Quebec, France's principal stronghold in the Western Hemisphere, and the accession of Carlos III, the ablest king since Philip II, to the Spanish throne. The second of these events tended to offset the results of the first. The continued English successes and French disasters of 1760 alarmed Carlos, and in 1761 he renewed the Family Compact and entered the war as the ally of France. In response to the challenge, in August, 1762, an English force captured Havana. Two months later another took Manila. The treaty of peace which closed the Seven Years' War restored the Philippines and Cuba to Spain, but gave Florida to England. By a secret treaty, signed before the conclusion of the war, France had transferred Louisiana to Spain to save it from England.

During its brief term under British rule and free

trade Havana prospered as never before; and Carlos was not slow to profit by the hint. Carlos indeed saw that to preserve his overseas domain and to restore Spain to her former eminence drastic reforms were necessary. From the last days of Philip II, Spain's power in Europe had declined, though her colonies had expanded in extent and population. The policy of absolutism was bearing fruit; and the harvest was ruin. While vast expenditures of men and money were being made in the conquest of new lands, the nation at home was being mangled under the weight of abnormal taxation. Industry could not survive and, therefore, a sturdy normal growth was impossible. The galleons brought gold, but it was spent in other than Spanish markets. The colonies produced far below their capacity because of the jealous restrictions imposed on them, and were further hampered by grafting officials. These were some of the external evidences of a blight that went deeper. Spain had kept the minds of her people dark in a day when other nations, accepting the challenge of new forces, were working out the principles of constitutional government and of individual liberty. In clinging to a selfish and fictitious ideal and in forcibly molding her people to it, she deprived them of the power of initiative and of systematic labor — the power which is derived from hope and joy — and so rendered them incapable of intellectual supremacy in an age differentiated from its predecessors by greater freedom and spiritual enlightenment.

To make amends for the stupidity of his predecessors, Carlos put forth brave efforts. He lowered taxation and instituted measures for the equalization of government. He revived and fostered Spanish industries and built up the navy. In less than a decade after Carlos's accession, Spain's colonial trade tripled and the revenue from the Indies increased from five million to twelve million crowns. While he installed economic reforms at home and in the colonies, he reorganized the frontier defenses of New Spain, and under the press of danger from England and Russia he extended Spain's northern outposts into Louisiana and California. Not since the days of Cortés had Spain taken so long a forward step in expansion. If, with all his energy and foresight, Carlos failed to accomplish his larger aims, it was because he came too late. Spain's great opportunity had passed, and no stroke of magic could free her people from the lethargy into which they had fallen.

Spain acquired French Louisiana by necessity.

not by design. On October 9, 1762, Louis XV offered the region to Carlos, who at first rejected the gift. But he soon changed his mind, for the value of Louisiana as a buffer against England could not be overlooked. Carlos deferred actual occupation as long as possible; but when he saw England's outposts advanced to the Mississippi, her settlers pushing over the Alleghanies, and her "long hunters" actually crossing the Mississippi, he realized that it was time to act.

The ceded territory embraced New Orleans and the western watershed of the Mississippi River. Its total population, exclusive of Indians, was estimated at from eight to twelve thousand persons of whom over half were negro slaves. The principal settlements lay along the Mississippi, the lower Red, and the lower Missouri. The bulk of the population lay between New Orleans and Pointe Coupée; other important settlements in the lower district were Balize, Attakapa, Opelousas, Avoyelle, and Natchitoches. Farther up were the Arkansas Post, St. Charles, and Ste. Geneviève. To the west, on the principal streams, there were slender trading stations such as the Cadodacho Post, on Red River, and Fort Cavagnolle, near where Kansas City now stands. Still farther in the interior, beyond the pale of civilization, roamed renegade Frenchmen and half breeds, who, under the name of hunters, had become veritable outlaws   The principal occupations of the province were agriculture and the fur trade.   For horses, mules, and cattle, dependence was placed on commerce with the Indians and Spaniards of the west.   Most of the stock purchased from the Indians was stolen from the Spaniards, and most of the direct trade with Spaniards was contraband.

The inhabitants of Louisiana at this day combined Spartan simplicity with a touch of courtly grandeur.   An inventory made in 1769 of the bedroom furniture of Madame Villeré, wife of a leading citizen of New Orleans, is typical.   It lists a cypress bedstead, with a mattress of corn husks, and one of feathers on top; a corn husk bolster; a cotton counterpane of home manufacture; six cypress chairs, with straw seats; seven candlesticks with green wax candles.   The house, says Gayarré, "must have looked very much like one of those modest and unpainted little wooden structures which are, to this day [1851] to be seen in many parts of the banks of the river Mississippi, and in the Attakapas and Opelousas parishes.   They are tenements of the small planters who own only a few slaves, and they retain the appellation of *Maisons d'Acadiens*." But inside these humble dwellings one sometimes encountered manners that suggested the ease and grace of the salons of Europe.

News of the cession to Spain of the French possessions caused consternation and protest among the settlers. From the Illinois country some of the inhabitants, in their desire to escape English rule, crossed the Mississippi and settled at St. Louis, where La Clede had recently established a trading post. Those of lower Louisiana were quite as anxious to escape Spanish rule. And they made known their wishes right noisily. An assembly at New Orleans made up of delegates from all the lower parishes drew up a memorial to Louis XV and sent it to France; but, in spite of the aid of the aged Bienville, the prayer was in vain. Still the colonists hoped on, for no Spanish official had arrived.

Hopes were dashed when, on March 5, 1766, Juan Antonio de Ulloa arrived at New Orleans as first Spanish Governor. Ulloa, a man of nearly fifty, was already a well-known scientist and naval officer. As a youth of nineteen, then a naval lieutenant, he had been sent to Peru with a brilliant scientific expedition. In the course of his labors there he was twice called to Lima to defend the province against the English under Admiral Anson. On the way to Europe around the Horn thirteen years later, his vessel, after capture by the English, escaped and sailed to Canada, where Ulloa was captured again. Taken to England, Ulloa was there made a member of the Royal Society of London. On his return to Spain he had published his now famous reports of the scientific expedition.

Ulloa arrived at New Orleans in a storm which was prophetic of the trouble that lay before him. His instructions provided that as little change as possible should be made in the administration of the colony. It was to be kept distinct from the other Spanish colonies, independent of the Council of the Indies, and dependent directly on the King. He was accompanied by a full corps of officers for the new colony, but had only ninety soldiers, for Louis XV had promised Carlos that the French provincial soldiery, under Aubry, should remain in the province as long as they were needed. This was a fatal mistake. Carlos should have cleaned house and given Ulloa a fair chance, with men whom he could command.

Ulloa was coldly received in New Orleans and was soon up to his ears in trouble with the turbulent

and dissatisfied *habitants*. The fault was not
one-sided. Ulloa was haughty and was bored by
the simple people he had been sent to rule. He
snubbed the Superior Council, a body which had
thoroughly enjoyed a little authority. The French
soldiers refused to enter the Spanish service. In
vain both Ulloa and Aubry urged. Thereupon
Ulloa gave up the idea of taking formal possession
and ruled through Aubry, who continued to be
nominal head of Louisiana. Ulloa commanded and
Aubry executed. Ulloa held the purse, Aubry the
sword. At the old posts the French flag continued
to wave before the breeze. At the same time, Ulloa
sent his ninety men to erect new posts, at Balize,
at the Iberville River, opposite Natchez, and in
Missouri. Over these new posts the Spanish flag
was hoisted. It was an anomalous situation.

Ulloa made a census of the province and an extended tour of the settlements. At Natchitoches
he spent some time, inquiring into communication
with Texas and Mexico. Among numerous benevolent deeds Ulloa's succor of the needy Acadian
exiles in Louisiana was not the least. But even this
caused dissatisfaction.

With their patriotism the French citizens mixed
solicitude for pocketbook. When Ulloa arrived

Louisiana was flooded with paper money which had depreciated to a fourth of its face value. Ulloa generously agreed to redeem it at three-fourths its face value, but nothing less than one hundred per cent would quiet complaint. Orders soon came from Spain which interfered with the ancient methods of French and English importers. The merchants appealed to the Council and the orders were suspended. Ulloa gave new offense by exiling himself to live for seven months "in a miserable shed" at Balize. The discovery that the fifty-year-old scholar had been waiting there for his expected bride, the Peruvian Marchioness of Abrado, mollified no one, and, when they moved to New Orleans, the Governor's wife and her train of Peruvian girls shared the Governor's unpopularity.

The intolerable situation came to a head in the autumn of 1768. For some time a conspiracy, headed by several Frenchmen, had been brewing. There is some ground for thinking that the leaders of the uprising had been inspired by the hope that, by getting control of the government, they could evade their debts and otherwise improve their fortunes. Secret meetings were held at the house of an adventuress in the suburbs of New Orleans, while emissaries worked among the outlying settlements.

On the 27th of October the guns at the gates of the city were spiked and the planters and settlers entered the city as an armed mob. A council called by the insurgents decreed that the Spaniards should leave within three days. Aubry remained faithful to Ulloa and placed him in safety on a frigate in the river. But the mob cut the cables, and Ulloa, the Marchioness, and her Peruvian girls sailed to Havana. The interior posts held by the Spanish soldiery were now abandoned. "Thus was the revolution accomplished," says Gayarré. "A population, which hardly numbered eighteen hundred men able to carry arms, and which had in its bosom several thousands of black slaves, whom it was necessary to intimidate into subjection, had rebelled against the will of France, had flung the gauntlet at the Spanish monarchy, and was bearding a powerful nation."

From Havana Ulloa reported the rebellion to the Marquis of Grimaldi. This official remonstrated with France for not having punished the insolent delegates to the French court. "The loss of great interests is looked upon in Spain with indifference but it is not so with regard to insults and contumelies," he said. A Council of State was held, wherein the question was raised as to whether Louisiana should be retained or given back to France. But on this point there was no hesitation. Out of six opinions rendered, all but one were emphatically for retention. The general view was well stated by the Count of Aranda. "The more or less fertility and extent of Louisiana is not the principal question to be examined. But we ought to judge of the importance of that acquisition, from the fact that it extends over Mexican territories to the bank of the Mississippi, a well-known barrier and a distant one from the population of New Mexico, and that it furnishes us, through that river, with an indelible line of demarcation between our provinces and those of the English, which have been widened by their acquisition of our domain in Florida." This was the kernel of the matter. Just as when Carlos III had accepted the gift, Louisiana was needed as a barrier to the advancing English, who were already crossing the Alleghanies and had their outposts on the Mississippi River.

But there was also the matter of Spain's pride, which could not be overlooked. The Duke of Alva gave an opinion that "bears the stamp of the hereditary temper of that haughty and inflexible house." The King, he said, should send to Louisiana a man with forces necessary to subject the people and stamp out disorders. The government should be so centralized as to leave the people no chance for a repetition of such audacity. "But finally, what to my judgment, appears to be of more importance than all the rest is, that it be seen throughout the world, and particularly in America, that the king knows how, and is able, to repress any attempt whatever, derogatory to the respect due to the royal majesty." Louisiana must be made an example to the rest of Spanish America!

The man chosen for this grim task was Alejandro O'Reilly. Like many of Spain's prominent men in the eighteenth century, he was an Irishman by birth. When a youth he had gone to Spain and served in the Hibernian Regiment. In the War of the Austrian Succession he had received a wound from which he limped the rest of his days. After serving in the armies of Austria and France he again served Spain in the wars with Portugal. Having risen to the rank of Brigadier General, he was employed to drill the Spanish army in Austrian tactics. In 1763, at the age of twenty-seven, with the rank of Major General, he was sent to Havana to reëstablish the fortifications which the English had ruined. Returning to Spain he became Inspector General of the King's Infantry and was made a

count. In 1765, by his presence of mind, he saved
the life of King Carlos during an insurrection.

When the news came of Ulloa's ejection, O'Reilly
had been ordered to Havana and Mexico to review the troops, but his mission was now changed.
His new orders required him to equip an expedition in Havana, go to Louisiana, take possession, arrest and try the leaders of the uprising,
expel all dangerous subjects, and reorganize the
province. In case of resistance he was authorized
to use force. "But as the king, whose character is
well known, is always inclined to be mild and clem-
ent, he has ordered O'Reilly to be informed that
his will is that a lenient course be pursued in the
colony, and that expulsion from it be the only punishment inflicted on those who have deserved a
more severe one."

While the fate of Louisiana was being discussed
in Spain, in New Orleans the people gradually deserted their erstwhile noisy spokesmen and turned
to Aubry for protection. The leaders awaited developments in nervous suspense. On July 24, 1769,
the place was thrown into commotion by word
that O'Reilly had arrived at Balize with a formid-
able force. One of the leaders of the rebellion
stuck a white cockade in his hat, appeared in

the public square, and urged the people to resist. But it was all in vain. The rebellion had
faded out. Aubry urged submission. A messenger
came from O'Reilly, and some of the leading con-
spirators hastened down the river, tumbling over
each other to be first to explain themselves and
promise loyalty.

O'Reilly's gentle demeanor allayed their fears.
The Frenchmen were dined and went back "full of
admiration for his talents, and with good hopes
that their past faults shall be forgotten." On the
17th of August the Spanish fleet, full twenty-four
sails, appeared before New Orleans. Next day
O'Reilly limped ashore, followed by his entire force,
twenty-six hundred in number, and took formal
possession with impressive ceremony. The people
were both overawed and edified by the spectacle.
Five times the cry *Viva el Rey!* went up from the
Spanish throats, and five times it was echoed by
the French soldiery and the populace. All the
bells pealed forth, and Aubry handed to O'Reilly
the keys of the city. The *fleur-de-lis* came down
and the banner of Spain floated to the breeze.
O'Reilly then repaired to the cathedral, where the
solemn ceremony was ended with a *Te Deum*.

The day after the ceremony of taking possession,

O'Reilly gave a dinner, with great pomp, to Aubry, French and Spanish officials, and other important personages. Meanwhile he was taking testimony in secret. Of Aubry he requested and obtained a full report of all the seditious occurrences in the colony. Aubry's eager compliance with this request is one of the acts which has lessened his fame in the old French colony.

With the evidence now in hand, O'Reilly's mind was made up. Under various pretexts twelve leaders were called to his house, arrested, their swords taken away, and their property sequestrated. While this scene was being enacted the house was surrounded with grenadiers. All twelve prisoners were lodged in separate places of confinement, some in vessels on the river, some in well guarded houses. One of the twelve, Villeré, had formerly prepared to flee the province and had then changed his mind. Being imprisoned in a frigate, he died — some say of frenzy, others of a bullet fired by his jailers. To the twelve originally arrested Foucault and Braud were later added on the charge of printing the *Memorial of the Planters*, one of the seditious publications which had appeared. Foucault refused to answer to the Spanish authorities, and, at his own request, was sent back to France to be tried. On his arrival there he was thrown into the Bastile. Braud was released.

The arrests and Villeré's death caused renewed consternation, and numerous colonists planned to flee to the English in Florida. Everybody trembled for his safety. But O'Reilly reassured the populace by a proclamation declaring that only the leaders should be punished. The oath of allegiance was administered to the inhabitants of New Orleans and vicinity. People living in the interior were given opportunities later for this ceremony. Every one who so desired was given the option of returning to France. Most of the inhabitants took the oath and remained.

Now followed the trial of the arrested men, an event which left a profound impression in the colony. The prosecuting attorney, Don Felix del Rey, was a learned practitioner before the courts of Santo Domingo and Mexico, and later Viceroy of Mexico. The prisoners rested their defense on the ground that Spain had never taken possession of Louisiana, hence that Ulloa could not require their obedience. Del Rey concluded, in a lengthy argument, that the accused were guilty of rebellion. On the 24th of October the court rendered the verdict, and O'Reilly, as president, pronounced the

sentence. O'Reilly condemned Lafrénière, Noyan,
Caresse, Marquis, and Joseph Milhet "to the ordinary pain of the gallows."   The memory of Villeré, who had died in prison, he condemned "to be
held and reputed forever infamous."   Petit was
condemned to perpetual imprisonment, Doucet to
ten years, Boisblanc, Jean Milhet, and Poupet to six
years each. The property of each was confiscated,
all those imprisoned were to be banished on release,
and all seditious publications were to be burned by
the hangman.

The friends of the condemned appealed and
pleaded in vain, for O'Reilly was firm. The execution was set for the next day. But no hangman
could be found. The official executioner of the colony was a negro, and it was conceded that a white
man would be more suitable for the task under the
circumstances. But in spite of rewards offered none
could be found, and the firing squad was sub-
stituted for the hangman.   The execution took
place in the public square at three in the afternoon,
the 25th of October. Next day the seditious *Memorial of the Planters* was publicly burned.   Petit
and his companions were taken to Havana and imprisoned in Morro Castle. It is pleasant to record
that soon afterward all were pardoned by Carlos.

Aubry sailed for France, but never reached there, for he sank with his ship in the Garonne River — an act of retribution, some thought.

The Spanish commander has ever since been known in Louisiana as "Bloody O'Reilly."

Now for a third of a century Louisiana remained under Spanish rule. By 1770 the Spanish flag had been raised at all the interior posts, Ste. Geneviève, below St. Louis, being the last to haul down the *fleur-de-lis*. Having accomplished his *coup d'état*, O'Reilly was conciliatory and appointed numerous old French officers to important positions. Spanish law and administration were installed, though the French Black Code was retained. New Orleans was given a *cabildo*, whose old building is still one of the attractions of the "French" quarter. Indeed more than one so-called French relic of the old city is Spanish.

Having put things in order, O'Reilly left Luís de Unzaga in charge as Governor. He in turn was followed in 1776 by dashing young Bernardo de Gálvez. Unzaga had winked at the English smugglers who monopolized the trade of the lower Mississippi and who were pushing west among the tribes of the Gulf Coast. But Gálvez began his administration by swooping down upon the

English smugglers, eleven of whose vessels he seized. Nevertheless they continued their trade, if less openly than before. They worked among the coast tribes, reached Texas overland, ascended the Arkansas and Missouri rivers, and worked among the tribes of Iowa and Minnesota. Trade in Pawnee and Spanish horses extended even to Virginia; Governor Patrick Henry being among the purchasers of thoroughbred Spanish stock.

In the attempt to keep the English out of Louisiana, Spanish defense was concentrated on the line of the Mississippi. On the other hand, since Louisiana belonged to Spain, the defenses and the missions of the old Texas-Louisiana border were withdrawn. The few settlers who lived on the border in the Los Adaes district, some five hundred in number, were evicted and taken to San Antonio (1773). The expulsion of these simple folk from their settlement, already over half a century old, was one of the pathetic incidents of the American border, and reminds one of the expulsion of the Acadians from Nova Scotia a few years before. Some of the settlers, refusing to be evicted, fled to the woods or to the surrounding tribes. Some of them, after remaining at San Antonio a year, and living at a settlement on the Trinity River five years, in 1779 took advantage of a flood and Comanche raids, followed their doughty Creole leader, Gil Ybarbo, to Nacogdoches, and from there scattered eastward to their former homes. Today, round about Robeline in Louisiana, and San Augustine in Texas, their descendants still live the simple life of their ancestors.

Louisiana was Spain's first experience in North America in a colony previously occupied by Europeans, and in it many departures were made from her traditional system. This was especially true of her Indian policy. Instead of relying for control upon the time honored mission and presidio, Spain utilized the French traders already among the tribes. But, with Spain's characteristic paternalism, the service was reorganized and much improved. A regular corps of licensed traders was installed; vagabonds, outlaws, and unlicensed traders were driven from the tribes, presents were distributed annually, and medals of merit were given to the friendly chiefs. In the Spanish days fur traders arose, Frenchmen for the most part, whose names are immortal in the West. At New Orleans there were Piseros and St. Maxent; at Natchitoches, Le Blanc, La Mathe, and Bormé; at Nacogdoches, Gil Ybarbo; and at St. Louis, the

Chouteaus, the Robidoux, Lisa, and Clamorgan. St. Louis, the Arkansas Post, and Natchitoches became centers for distributing presents and holding councils with tribes living on both sides of the Mississippi River.

Of all the tribes none were more important than those of the Red River valley, in the present States of Louisiana, Texas, Arkansas, and Oklahoma. They had been friendly to the French and hostile to Spain, and it was necessary to win them to Spanish allegiance. This important task was assigned to Athanase de Mézières, an old French officer in the military service. In recognition of his ability as an Indian agent, O'Reilly had put him in charge of the district of Natchitoches. For ten years he labored loyally at his task. By eloquence, presents, and bluff, he induced most of the hostile tribes to make treaties. He toured their villages as far as the upper Brazos River, and thence marched south three hundred miles to San Antonio over an unknown trail. Six years later he was called to Texas to prepare the new allies for a great campaign of extermination against the Apaches, hated foes of both the Spaniards and Eastern tribes.

For several years after 1776 the vital question in

Louisiana was the outcome of the American Revolution. After long hesitation, in April, 1779, Spain at last joined the revolting colonies. Her primary aim was not popular liberty, but conquest at the expense of England, for she hoped to obtain Gibraltar, Minorca, the Floridas, British Honduras, and perhaps the country between the Alleghanies and the Mississippi. With lightning speed Gálvez, the youthful Governor of Louisiana, captured the English posts on the lower Mississippi. Two years later Mobile and Pensacola were at his feet. Meanwhile an English expedition from Canada against St. Louis by way of Wisconsin had failed (1780) and in retaliation a force from St. Louis had run up the Spanish flag at St. Joseph, Michigan. Spain had frustrated the British attempt to gain control of the Mississippi, had enabled George Rogers Clark to hold his conquests in the Illinois, and had recovered Florida. Her Anglo-American frontier now stretched all the way from St. Mary's River on the Atlantic coast to the head of the Mississippi.

Spain's rule in Louisiana added to her already long and illustrious list of trailmakers. Communication for defense and trade had to be opened between Louisiana and the old outposts of New Spain and, at the same time, between San Antonio and

Santa Fé, which had been cut off from each other by the intervening Apaches and Comanches. The principal agent in this work was Pedro Vial. Vial was sent in 1786 from San Antonio to find a direct route to Santa Fé. In spite of a fall from his horse, with one companion he made his way to Red River; thence westward through the Comanche country to Santa Fé. He had found the Comanches friendly, but his route was roundabout. José Mares found a more direct trail to San Antonio (1787) while Vial explored from Santa Fé, down the Red and Sabine rivers, to Natchitoches, returning thence to San Antonio and to Santa Fé by a still more direct route than that of Mares. On the journey he had traveled farther than from Chicago to San Francisco. This tireless pathfinder next explored from Santa Fé to St. Louis (1792) returning by a route approximating that of the later Santa Fé Trail. He had preceded Pike by fifteen years. He was not a great diarist, but he was a good frontiersman.

What Mézières and Vial had done in lower Louisiana, Clamorgan and his associates now did in upper Louisiana. Americans from the Ohio Valley and Scotch traders from Canada were invading the country in growing numbers. Making their way by the Des Moines, the St. Peters, and the Assiniboine rivers, they traded and even built posts among the Omahas, Arikaras, and Mandans. At the same time Russians and British were threatening the Oregon coast. To ward off these dangers, in 1793 the "Company of Explorers of the Missouri" was chartered at St. Louis. A prize of $2000 was offered to the first person who should reach the Pacific by way of the Missouri. Now there was a spurt of energy, and by 1797 Trudeau, Lecuyer, Mackay, and Evans, in the service of Clamorgan's Company, had carried the Spanish flag above the Mandan villages in North Dakota. But the ambitious schemes of the Company were not realized. The Government failed to pay Clamorgan the promised annual subsidy of $10,000 and rival traders opposed the Company's monopoly. The St. Louis trade, however, continued to develop, and Lewis and Clark in 1804 found traces of Spaniards far up Cheyenne River.

American traders invaded upper Louisiana and the backwoodsmen pressed upon the lower Mississippi frontier. To hold them back, Spain intrigued and employed Indian agents, like Alexander McGillivray of West Florida. Spain denied to the backwoodsmen the right to navigate the

Mississippi, but they protested, intrigued, made reprisals, and appealed to the Government, till in 1795 their point was gained through diplomacy. Still they kept pressing on across the Mississippi. To check their advance, Spain imported Canary Islanders and invited British Loyalists to settle. Finally she tried counter-colonies formed of the Americans themselves. Thus in 1790 Colonel George Morgan crossed over and founded New Madrid. Before the end of the century scores of other Americans, among them Moses Austin and Daniel Boone, had been given liberal Spanish grants in the vain hope that they would hold back their brethren. By the opening of the new century the population of Louisiana had reached fifty thousand, as against some ten thousand at the end of the French régime, and a large part of the increase was due to American immigration.

Napoleon needed Louisiana for his own purposes, and in 1800 he took it. Three years later with as little ceremony he sold it to the United States. Spain now fell back again on her old Texas and New Mexico frontier, where the struggle with the Anglo-Americans was renewed. They pushed on across Louisiana into Texas. Horse drovers and traders, like Philip Nolan, operated in Texas from the time of the American Revolution. Early in the nineteenth century adventurers like Aaron Burr and James Wilkinson laid plans for filibustering raids. During the Mexican War of Independence Americans led expeditions into Texas to aid in the struggle for liberty, while others crowded over the borders and settled on the bottom lands along the Red and Sabine rivers. When Mexico won independence from Spain in 1821, Austin and a host of others obtained princely grants of rich Texas soil. Fifteen years later the American settlers revolted and set up a republic, which, after nine proud years of independence was annexed to the United States. War with Mexico followed, and in 1848 New Mexico, Arizona, Colorado, Utah, Nevada, and California went the way of Texas. Five years afterwards, the Gadsden Purchase added to the United States another slice of the old Spanish domain. From Jamestown (1607) to the Gadsden Purchase (1853) is a continuous story of the pressure of Anglo-Americans upon Hispanic borderlands not effectively occupied. On the south the American tide stopped at the Río Grande, finding there a bulwark of substantial settlement.

CHAPTER X

CALIFORNIA

THE English had made the occupation of Louisiana imperative. Carlos lifted his eyes to the West, and there he saw another menace. Russian fur hunters had overrun Siberia to the Pacific by the beginning of the eighteenth century. Catherine of Russia, continuing the age-old quest for the Strait of Anian, in 1725 had sent Vitus Bering, the Dane, to seek a northern passage from the Pacific into the Atlantic. On his first voyage (1725–1730) he discovered Bering Strait, leading, not into the Atlantic, but into the Arctic Ocean, where Siberia and Alaska all but touch hands. By the close of the Seven Years' War Russian fur-trading posts had been established on Bering, Kadiak, and Unalaska Islands, and Russian vessels were cruising Pacific waters southward toward Oregon. Moreover, there was the perilous prospect of an English incursion overland from Canada or from the Ohio Valley.

California had been in danger before, and little had been done. The Russian menace might have ended with correspondence had there not been on the frontier a man of action clothed with ample powers. This man was José de Gálvez, the visitor-general who had carried out for Carlos reforms in New Spain. Gálvez not only realized that a crisis had arrived but, true to form, he acted; and, while settling affairs in Lower California, he organized a defensive expedition to Alta California. The plan was typical of Spain's method of holding and as-similating new frontiers. Soldiers and missionaries were to go forth, side by side, and plant military colonies and missions at San Diego and Monterey, then the most celebrated harbors on the coast, for the Bay of San Francisco was still unknown.

To carry out the work Gálvez had good material ready at hand. The general command was entrusted to Don Gaspar de Portolá, the newly appointed Governor of Lower California. Since the expulsion of the Jesuits, the work of converting and civilizing the natives there had devolved upon a band of Fran-ciscan friars, sons of the missionary college of San Fernando, at Mexico City. The president of these "Fernandinos" in Lower California, Fray Juní-pero Serra, was chosen to guide the banner of the

Faith into the new territory, and he would take with him five other friars chosen from his missions. The expedition, which was under way early in 1769, consisted of two passenger vessels and a supply ship and two overland parties.

Owing to errors in latitude made by the earlier explorers, the vessels sailed too far north in their search for San Diego Bay. The *San Antonio* reached port after fifty-four days at sea. The *San Carlos* was one hundred and ten days on the way, and when she entered the harbor her crew were too ill from scurvy and lack of fresh water to lower the boats. A fortnight was spent chiefly in caring for the sick and burying the dead. The supply ship, the *San José*, was never heard of again after her departure from port in Lower California.

The land expeditions were much more fortunate, though the way was difficult and long. Provisions for the journey, horses, mules, and cattle were assembled at Velicatá, a post eighteen leagues beyond Santa María, the northernmost of the old missions.

The first of the overland parties set out from Velicatá on March 24, 1769. It was led by Captain Rivera, commander of the company of Loreto. He had twenty-five leather jacket soldiers (*soldados de cuera*), three muleteers, and some forty Indians

from the old missions, equipped with pick, shovel,
ax, and crowbar, to open the roads through the
mountains and across gullies. Along went Father
Juan Crespi, principal historian of the expedition.
Rivera's men were declared to be "the best horsemen in the world, and among those soldiers who
best earn their bread from the august monarch
whom they serve." The *cuera*, which gave them
their name, was a leather jacket, like a coat without sleeves, reaching to the knees, and made of six
or seven plies of white buckskin, proof against the
Indians' arrows except at very close range. For
additional armor they had shields and chaps. The
shields, carried on the left arm, were made of two
plies of bull's hide, and would turn either arrow or
spear. The leather chaps or aprons, fastened to the
pommel of the saddle, protected legs and thighs
from brush and cactus spines.

For the first eight days the trail was that followed by the Jesuit Father Linck, three years before. Thereafter, a distance of three hundred miles,
the route was now explored by white men for the
first time. Frequently water had to be carried in
barrels and skin bags (*botas*), for the Peninsula is
dry. More than once the animals had to camp for
the night without water. Sometimes there was no

fuel for a camp fire. Several nights were made terrible by the roaring of a lion. Much of the way was over rugged mountains. The wild Indians did no harm, but they were occasionally threatening. Frequently it rained, and the men spent uncomfortable nights in water-soaked clothing. At last the difficult journey came to an end. On the 13th of May, scouts from a height saw the masts of the two vessels anchored in San Diego Bay. Next day their joy was mixed with sadness; the welcome salutes and the fond embraces were offset by the sad news of the horrible inroads made by scurvy into the ranks of the sea party.

On the 15th of May, the day after Rivera and Crespi reached San Diego, Portolá and Serra set out from Velicatá. The season was better, the trail had been broken, and the journey was quicker than Rivera's. On the last day of June, after a march of six weeks, the wayfarers reached San Diego. Serra said Mass, the *Te Deum* was sung, and artillery roared salute from the new outpost of Church and State. The first band of Spanish pioneers on the soil of Alta California, when all were assembled, comprised one hundred and twenty-six souls; ninety-three of the original number had perished on the *San Carlos* or after landing;

of the Indians, some had deserted on the way, reluctant to leave home. On Sunday, the 16th of July, Serra preached to a group of natives made happy by little trinkets from his stock, and dedicated the mission of San Diego de Alcalá. Nearby the presidio of San Diego was founded.

The port of Monterey was still to be protected. Portolá therefore sent the *San Antonio* back to Mexico for men and supplies; then, leaving the *San Carlos* at anchor for want of a crew, he continued up the coast by land to complete his task, without the aid of the vessels. The march began on the 14th of July, two days before Serra formally founded his mission of San Diego. Ahead rode Portolá, Fages, Costansó, the friars, six Catalan volunteers, and the Indian sappers. Next followed the pack train in four divisions, each of twenty-five loaded mules, with muletcers and a soldier guard. In the rear came Captain Rivera, the rest of the soldiers, and friendly Indians driving the herd of spare mules and horses.

Portolá and his band rode northward along the coast by a route practically that now followed by the railroads. Most of the way pasture and water were plentiful and the Indians numerous and friendly. At Los Angeles River a sharp earthquake shock was felt. "It lasted about half as long as an Ave María, and about ten minutes later it was repeated, though not so violently." The coast was followed without great difficulty past San Luís Obispo to a point near the southern line of Monterey County. Here the way was blocked by rugged Santa Lucía Mountain, whose steep cliffs overhang the sea. A halt of several days was necessary for Rivera and the scouts to find a way through the mountains. The march was continued then to the north and northeast for about forty-five miles across Nacimiento and San Antonio rivers, and down Arroyo Seco to Salinas River, which was reached near Soledad. It was one of the hardest stretches of country encountered by the early explorers of the West. Crespi wrote, "The mountains . . . are inaccessible not only for men but also for goats and deer." Arroyos flowing down the gorges had to be crossed innumerable times. From a high peak near San Antonio River nothing but mountains could be seen in any direction. "It was a sad spectacle for us, poor wayfarers, tired and worn out by the fatigues of the long journey." Some of the soldiers by now were disabled by scurvy. "All this tended to oppress our hearts; but, remembering the object to which these toils were directed, and that it was for the greater glory of God through the conversion of souls, and for the service of the king, whose dominions were being enlarged by this expedition, all were animated to work cheerfully."

Six days down Salinas River took the expedition to the shore of Monterey Bay. But Vizcaíno had told of a "fine harbor." None was found, and Portolá, mystified, concluded that some mistake had been made, and that the harbor must be farther north. He therefore continued up the coast. As the men pressed on through the spacious forests, they saw, rank upon rank, the sheer, ruddy trunks of giant timber, and they called this new tree the *palo colorado*. This is the first historical mention of the famous California redwood. At Half Moon Bay they saw the Farallones, Point Reyes, and Drake's Bay; which last they recognized at once, for it was better known than any other point on the north coast. Plainly, they had passed Monterey and were a long distance out of their course. So they pitched camp at Point Pedro, to rest and to debate what should be done. And, their food being nearly exhausted, some hunters struck into the mountains northeast of the camp to look for game. The chase, or perhaps only the hope of it, led them upward until presently they came out on a clear height and beheld a great quiet harbor, almost land-locked, so near together stood the two titanic pillars of its one gate, open to the sunset ocean. These hunters were the first white men to catch a glimpse of San Francisco Bay.

On the 4th of November, Portolá's party descended to the bay and explored it to its head. Then, retracing their route along the coast, they again reached Point Pinos and Monterey Bay They planted two crosses, one on Carmel River and the other on the bay shore, and continued on to San Diego.

There affairs had gone badly. Fifty persons had died and the rest were homesick. During Portolá's absence they had had a serious brush with the natives, who had pillaged their huts and stripped the invalids of their garments. Provisions were scarce, and there was even talk of abandoning the enterprise. But Rivera was dispatched to Loreto for stock and supplies, and the pioneers held on as if they knew the full meaning of their fortitude. In the crisis Serra's faith was superb. "What I have desired least is provisions," he wrote. "Our needs are many, it is true; but if we have health, a tortilla, and some vegetables, what more do we want?

. . . If I see that along with the food hope vanishes I shall remain along with Father Juan Crespi and hold out to the last breath."

But relief was at hand. To the eyes of the friars, who had kept an unceasing vigil of prayer for nine days, and to the discouraged Portolá, the white sails of the *San Antonio* cleaving the clear blue twilight must have seemed as the wings of some heavenly visitant, more beautiful than ever ship before had spread to the beneficent wind. Alta California had been saved from the danger of abandonment. Another expedition to Monterey was successful and the presidio and mission of San Carlos were founded there (1770), near the spot where one hundred and sixty-eight years before Father Ascensión had said Mass under a spreading oak tree.

The Russian menace had been met. Spain's frontier had been advanced eight hundred miles. That the event was of more than local import was generally felt, and the news of it, hurried to Mexico by special courier and dispatch boat, was celebrated at the capital. "His Excellency [the Viceroy] wanted the whole population forthwith to share in the happiness which the information gave him, and therefore he ordered a general ringing of the bells of the cathedral and all the other churches, in order that all might realize the importance of the Port of Monterey to the Crown of our monarch, and also to give thanks for the happy success of the expeditions; for by their means the dominion of our king had been extended over more than three hundred leagues of good land." More than this, the Viceroy ordered a solemn Mass of thanksgiving sung in the cathedral, and attended in person with his whole viceregal court.

Two problems of major importance now engaged the authorities — the opening of a land route from Sonora and the occupation of San Francisco Bay. Thus far supplies had been sent chiefly by ship from San Blas to Loreto on the peninsula, thence northward by pack train over seven hundred and fifty miles of largely arid country to San Diego and five hundred and fifty miles farther to Monterey. California needed colonists, and the supply ships were too small to transport them in any number. The soldiers in California, left without their families, chose their companions from among the native women and thus grievously hampered the work of the friars. Furthermore, a land route would reduce the cost of the new settlements to the government by opening a way for the transport of stock and crops raised abundantly in Sonora.

The man for the task was found in Juan Bautista de Anza, commander of Tubac, an Arizona fort, and a frontiersman by birth and training. Anza set out from his post at Tubac with a company of thirty-four men, including two friars, thirty-five mules laden with provisions, sixty-five cattle, and one hundred and forty horses — the horses being poor animals, as the best of the stock had just been run off by the Apaches. He turned southwest, crossed the divide, and descended the Altar River through the Pima missions to Caborca, the last Spanish settlement between Sonora and Father Serra's San Gabriel Mission, six hundred miles distant. From Caborca his way led through the Pápago country to the Gila at the Colorado Junction, over the waterless Devil's Highway, where men and beasts suffered torture from thirst. At the junction he made friends with Palma, chief of the Yumas, and presented him with a bright sash and a necklace of coins struck with the King's image, which latter so delighted the naked giant that "he neither had eyes enough to look at it, nor words with which to express his gratitude." The Yumas assisted Anza in crossing the Colorado River and guided him down its farther bank to Santa Olaya Lake, on the edge of the great sand dunes of the Colorado Desert.

His guides from here forward were Father Francisco Garcés, who three years before had crossed the Colorado Desert, and Sebastian, an Indian who had fled east across the Sierras from Mission San Gabriel to Sonora. But the guides lost their way and for about a fortnight Anza wandered helplessly among the dunes till at last he encountered mountains of sand which the jaded animals would not even attempt to pass. When he turned back towards Santa Olaya Lake his difficulties were not over; for the blowing sand had wiped out all trails. But at last he reached it and there went into camp for two weeks, to rest and restore the men and the pack animals. The camp was thronged daily with the Yumas and their allies. The friars, Fathers Díaz and Garcés, endeavored to convert the savages; and the soldiers, who had a fiddler among them, held nightly dances with the Indian girls, there on the rim of the desert, defying its menace with their jollity.

Anza left a part of his equipment and some of his men with the Yumas and went on with the others, who had sworn to persevere with him to the end.

even if they should have to make the coast on foot.
He went southwestward, down the Colorado, seek-
ing a way round the southern line of the desert.
He found water and pasturage north of the Cócopa
Mountains, from which point he veered generally
northwestward to a pass in the Sierra Nevada
Mountains.

This trail of the first white man to cross the
Sierras is historic. Anza entered the great range
by way of San Felipe Creek. "The canyon is
formed by several very high, rocky mountains, or it
would be better to say, by great heaps of rocks and
stones of all sizes, which look as though they had
been gathered and piled there, like the sweepings of
the world." Continuing up Coyote Canyon, past
starved Indians living in the cliffs and caves "like
rabbit warrens," three days after leaving the desert
he emerged through a rocky pass into Cahuilla
Valley.[1] The desert now gave way to mountain
verdure. "At this very place," says Anza, "there
is a pass which I named Royal Pass of San Carlos.
From it are seen some most beautiful valleys, very

[1] Not Hemet Valley as is generally held. In August, 1920, the
author and Mr. W. G. Paden, by a personal reconnaissance on the
ground, demonstrated this error. The rocky pass, called San
Carlos, today opens into the corral of Rancho de la Puerta,
owned by Mr. Fred Clark.

green and flower strewn; snowy mountains with live oaks and other trees native to cold lands. The waters, too, are divided, some running on this side to the Gulf, and others to the Philippine Ocean." Anza crossed the plateau, a distance of some fifteen miles, and, little hindered by falling snow on the mountains, which turned to mist in the valley, descended Bautista Canyon and camped on San Jacinto River. A few days later, as the Southern California sunset blazed upon the peaks, Anza knocked at the gates of San Gabriel Mission, near the future Los Angeles. His march had covered some seven hundred miles. He went on to Monterey and returned from there to Tubac over the trail which he had opened, through the Royal Pass of San Carlos.

The Golden Gate could now be protected. Having first been to Mexico City to confer with Viceroy Bucarely, on October 23, 1775, Anza led out from the rendezvous at Tubac the first colony destined for San Francisco. It comprised soldiers, friars, and thirty families — in all two hundred and forty persons. The type of Spanish colonist to be had is amply revealed in Anza's recommendations to the authorities. Their pay must be given them in advance, because most of them were "submerged in poverty," and it must be given to them in the form of clothing and outfit because, if paid in money, they would immediately gamble it all away. The list of essentials included — besides arms, horses, mules, cattle, and rations — shirts, underwear, jackets, breeches, hose, buckskin boots and buttoned shoes, capes, hats, and handkerchiefs for the men, also ribbons for their hats and their hair; for the women, chemises, petticoats, jackets, shoes, stockings, hats, *rebozos* and ribbons; and the items of children's needs also concluded with ribbons. Spurs, bridle and bit, saddle and saddle-cushion, and a leathern jacket (*cuera*) of seven thicknesses, were a few more of each man's requirements. And the dole of each family seems to have included all inventions known at the time from frying pans to blank books! Two hundred head of cattle were taken to stock California. In the party were three friars, Font, Garcés, and Eixarch. Garcés, who had accompanied Anza to San Gabriel on his first journey, and Eixarch, were to remain with the Yuma Indians at the mouth of the Gila. Font went as diarist and astronomer. The Gila was reached on the 28th of November without other grave mishap than the death of a woman in childbirth. Six days were spent at Yuma, the junction

of the Gila and the Colorado, because of illness
among the women, and because of the necessity of
installing Garcés and Eixarch among their chosen
flock.   Anza ordered a cabin erected for the friars and their servants and stocked it with provisions for four months.   Chief Palma aided with
all the weight of his great authority.   Such was the
beginning of white settlement at Yuma.

On the 4th of December Anza resumed his journey.   Some of his horses had died from the cold,
and there were eleven sick persons in the party.
At Santa Olaya Lake he divided his expedition into
three relays, to march on different days, in order to
save the scant water holes in the desert country
ahead.   In his conferences with Palma, whom he
had now rendered ecstatic by the gift of a Spanish
military costume, Anza must have learned more
about the way over the sand dunes; for, leading the
first detachment in person, he struck out straight
ahead across the desert.   In three days he reached
the cool wells of Santa Rosa, and, two days later,
camped at San Sebastián, near the pass into the
mountains.   Here he awaited the remainder of his
party.   When the other detachments came up, the
colonists were ill from cold and thirst, and the two
hundred cattle had been without water for four

days. The horses were badly worn. Just before
leaving Tubac the Apaches had stolen fifteen hundred head, and most of the emigrants had come
without change of mounts, in some cases with
two or three children on a single horse. Hence-
forth some went on foot. But human nature is
buoyant. And the reunion at San Sebastián was
celebrated with a noisy dance. A bold widow
sang a naughty song; her paramour punished her;
Anza reprimanded the man, and Father Font
reproved Anza.

Anza's cavalcade turned northwestward now
and crossed the Sierras by way of the path he had
discovered on his former journey. The snow-cov-
ered mountains extended a chilly reception to the
colonists, who came from semi-tropical Sonora and
Sinaloa. The women wept, but Anza dried their
tears. In the deep canyon on Christmas eve, a
child was born, the third extra colonist to enter the
ranks of the expedition since the departure from
Tubac. On the way up the mountain slope over
ninety head of cattle died from cold and exhaus-
tion. Just at San Carlos Pass a severe earthquake
shock was experienced by the weary band. The
intrepid Anza — Tomiár, or Big Chief, the Cahuil-
las called him — had intended to break trail from

the pass to Monterey without touching at San Gabriel, but the condition of his party and the stock made this plan impracticable. Where Riverside now stands he crossed the Santa Ana River on the bridge built by himself two years before and led his colonists into the precincts of San Gabriel on January 4, 1776. Two months later he had brought them to Monterey.

Anza explored the shores of San Francisco Bay and selected sites for a presidio and a mission and then returned to Sonora. The march of over a thousand miles, which he had led, was one of the longest overland migrations of a colony in North American history before the settlement of Oregon.

It is worthy of note that even while Don Juan Anza reconnoitered San Francisco Bay for a site whereon to erect the outward signs of absolute monarchy, the Liberty Bell at Philadelphia three thousand miles away proclaimed the signing of the Declaration of Independence; and that within seventy-five years San Francisco was to become the western gateway of the new American nation.

The presidio of San Francisco was founded in September and the mission in October, 1776. Next year one of Anza's lieutenants founded San José, some miles to the south, close to the mission of

Santa Clara. Four years later a second body of colonists came over Portolá's route and founded the pueblo of Los Angeles. The year 1782 saw the founding of Santa Bárbara. Thus Spain had made good her hold on California at four strategic points, San Diego, Santa Bárbara, Monterey, and San Francisco, having meanwhile pushed exploration by sea up the present Oregon and British Columbia coasts with an eye always to Russian and English activities. Spain was much disturbed to find that England, who should have been fully occupied with the Revolutionary War in America and the defense of her frontiers from the English Channel to India against the combined power of France and Spain, had yet found time to send an explorer, Captain Cook, into North Pacific waters.[1]

Of names illustrious in the pioneer mission field of America none is more renowned than Junípero Serra. If, as in the case of Serra, we are disposed to think that the biographies of some of the pioneer padres, written by members of their own Order, may be too colored with hero worship to be strictly historical, let us remember at the same time that only men capable of arousing exalted affection

[1] See *Adventurers of Oregon* in this Series.

and admiration could tempt their memorialists into this extravagance. In his character, it is plain, Serra was gentle, loving, and selfless. Like Kino, he had distinguished himself in the Old World and had turned his back upon honors to enter the laborious and perilous life of a missionary to savages. It was a life that promised little but hardship, disappointment, danger, to be cut short, perhaps, by a death of agony at the hands of those he sought to save. Whatever might be the worldly policies of governors and ecclesiastics pertaining to the results of his labors, the true missionary himself was moved by two separate motives — a passion for his Faith and a yearning towards those whom he deemed eternally lost without it. His humanity as well as his zeal found exercise in a fatherly interest in the children of the wilderness and in efforts to teach them innocent games and pleasures in the place of some of their native amusements which were less moral. To learn their various languages — and Indian languages are among the most difficult to master — to coax them into habits of industry, to make them love labor and strict virtue as well as the Catechism — required infinite patience and kindness no less than a heart staunch against all fear.

Such a blend of zeal and humanity was seen in Junípero Serra. Withal, he was an organizer and executive. All in all, indeed, Serra was the outstanding Spanish pioneer of California. During the fifteen years of his labors there, he supervised the founding of nine permanent missions of the twenty-one which the Franciscans built in the Golden State before secularization undid the work of their Order.[1] San Diego was the first, but the more famous was San Carlos at Carmel, where Serra lived until his death in 1784. The present San Carlos, which has been preserved and is still regularly used for services, was begun on the same site in 1793. The little congregation which gathers there now answers no longer to the descriptions left us by visitors of long ago — such as those of the Frenchman La Pérouse, who saw the original building, the English discoverer, George Vancouver, and, later, the Boston seaman and writer, Richard Henry Dana. Then, along the five-mile road

[1] San Diego, 1769; San Carlos, 1770; San Gabriel, 1771; San Antonio de Padua, 1771; San Luis Obispo, 1772; San Juan Capistrano, 1776; San Francisco de Assisi, 1776; Santa Clara, 1777; San Buenaventura, 1782; Santa Bárbara, 1786; La Purísima Concepción, 1787; Santa Cruz, 1791; Soledad, 1791; San Juan Bautista, 1797; San Fernando, 1797; San Miguel, 1797; San José, 1797; San Luís Rey, 1798; Santa Inez, 1804; San Rafael, 1817; San Francisco Solano, 1823.

leading from Monterey, the capital, to Carmel,
passed the magnificent Governor and his uniformed
escort, *caballeros* in slashed and gilt-laced pantaloons and brilliant *serapes*, staid *señoras* shrouded
in black lace mantillas yet keeping an eye on their
daughters, whose glances, decorous but eager, roved
over the rim of the cart as some hero with jingling
spurs curvetted past, peasants under their huge
sombreros, gray-gowned friars in sandals, Indian
muleteers and *vaqueros*, and Indian laborers in their
coarse dull cotton smocks. Scarlet, gold, and blue
livened the black and white and tawny brown in
the costuming of this frequent procession, which
made its way along the shore of a sea sapphire and
amethyst and spread with the hammered gold of
the kelpfields, on through the green slopes, on
among the giant columns of the Carmel pines, to
San Carlos, on the hill above the river, with red-
tiled roof and belfry and thick bluish stone walls.
In Serra's day there was only a small adobe church
beside the orchards of olives and fruit trees which
he planted. Half a stone's throw from the church
Serra dwelt in a cell furnished with a chair and a
table, a bed of boards, and the blanket which covered him when he slept. Nearby rose a high cross
and, at dawn and often through the day and night,

he knelt at its foot in prayer. It was, says Father Palou, Serra's pupil, friend, and biographer, "his companionship and all his delight." Under the shadow of the cross in his cell, attended by his disciple Palou, Serra died. From near and far, the Indians who venerated him came to strew his plain coffin with flowers. And they wept bitterly that their Padre, now silent in death, would never again greet them with his habitual tender admonition, "*amar á Dios*" — to love God.

Aided by other devoted Franciscans, Serra had accomplished much according to the plan which he held to be essential to the welfare of the Indians. Along the fertile coast valleys from San Diego to San Francisco stretched a chain of missions, some seated so that the limits of one mission's lands touched upon the borders of the next. Grain fields, vineyards, olive groves, and orchards flourished, cared for by native labor under Indian overseers. Indian herdsmen tended the great flocks of sheep and the droves of cattle and horses. Each mission with its lands and its Indians formed a type of patriarchal state under the padre's rule backed by the soldiery. Under the new régime, which curbed every native instinct and changed the whole fashion of their lives the Indians decreased. But, while

it is easy to pick flaws in the mission system of deal-
ing with the Indians, it is not so easy to point to
any other system which has done better. The
problem of civilizing a wild people has baffled
others than the padres.

In the policy of the Government regarding the
missions and in the plans of the friars, the Indian
was the central idea. Both looked to his conversion and civilization. The Government intended, after a reasonable period, to take over the
missions, turn them into pueblos under civil juris-
diction, each church to become a curacy of the
diocese, and to allot land to the Indians, who were
to be no longer neophytes under patriarchal domi-
nance, but citizens living independent lives under
the rule of the state. The mission lands did not
belong to the friars, whose vows of poverty pre-
cluded their holding property. The usufruct was
theirs to manage, as stewards and administrators
salaried by the Crown but having themselves no
titles to the occupied territory. The friars were
not in sympathy with the governmental desire pre-
maturely to secularize the missions and thus to expel the missionaries, or to confine the activities of
those who might remain to purely spiritual affairs. It is conceivable that they did not wish to

resign their temporal powers; and it is certain that they did not believe that the Indians would be benefited by the change. With all their energy, therefore, the friars resisted secularization.

A decree passed by the Spanish Cortés in 1813, but not published in California until January, 1820, ordered the friars immediately to "cease from the government and administration of the property" of the Indians; but a vigorous controversy halted its execution. After the revolt from Spain, the Mexican Government enacted laws of the same tenor, looking, as some say, to the emancipation of the Indians and to their participation in the life of the state as citizens, or, as others put it, to the confiscation of the mission lands. The immediate result was confusion, waste, and destruction. The Indians did not comprehend the new measures, said to be designed for their progress. They accepted the views of the friars that a great evil was being committed by the new republican Government. To oppose that Government some at least of the mission Indians had been armed and drilled under the direction of their padres, whose sympathies were strongly royalist. Not understanding that the lands and herds which they had tended were now legally to become their own, and believing only that they and their padres were to be robbed of them, they plunged into a furious destruction of live stock and other property. Helpless to cope with the situation, the new Government ordered a temporary restoration of the old system. But the trouble did not abate. Dishonest officials, eager only to possess themselves of the valuable lands destined for the Indians, added to the complexity of the problem. Settlers intruded into the mission valleys and took up holdings. Natives helped themselves to stock and ran off to distant rancherías. By 1843, five of the missions at least had been entirely deserted. In 1845 a proclamation provided for the rental or sale of the missions. The abandoned buildings were to be sold at auction. The surplus property of others was to be sold and the buildings rented. This order had not been fully carried out when the flag of the United States was raised at Monterey on July 7, 1846. Under American regulations, the mission buildings with an adequate amount of land were restored to the Church. The surplus land reverted to the Government. So, in the end, the Indians possessed nothing. Retreating before the inrush of white settlers, they went back to their wild life, far less able to cope with its conditions after some fifty years of civilization and strict religious discipline. A few of the friars remained till they died to care for the spiritual welfare of their scattered and diminished flocks. The majority departed for other mission fields or returned to their monasteries in Mexico and Europe.

The missions, some of them intact, others in various stages of decay, or of restoration through the activities of the Landmarks Club of California, remain as monuments, not alone to the friars who designed them, but also to the Indians who built them. The natives, instructed by their padres, made those adobe bricks and quarried those great stone blocks and piled them into the high walls several feet in thickness, into the tall pillars, the rounded arches, the belfry towers and the solid courtyards of buildings covering, in some instances, enormous sites. San Luís Rey, the largest of the missions, built of adobe, had a corridor of thirty-two broad arches opening upon its *patio*, which was about eighty yards square. Nearly three thousand Indians peopled the adjacent village, tilled the mission's lands and herded its stock; and, in the evenings, a native band of forty pieces played for the delectation of their tribesmen and their padres. The Indians built roads and bridges under the tutelage of the friars, some of whom had been architects and engineers, prior to taking vows Indians baked the dusky red tiles for the roofs. They carved the altar pieces and pulpits, the doorposts and lintels; they made the moldings and employed their primitive native art in the brilliantly colored frescoes which still adorn some of the interior walls. They hewed and smoothed the great beams for the ceilings and grooved them into place; and they wrought the stone bowls for font and fountain and set them on their adobe pedestals. Patient teaching and faithful labor wrought for beauty and God.

The architecture combined something of the Moresque, the Roman, and the Old Spanish, and was perhaps influenced by the Aztec, certainly was influenced by the needs and inspirations and the climatic conditions of a virgin country and by the materials at hand for building. The result was an original style, massively beautiful and harmonious with the landscape. Santa Barbara is a famous example. It never suffered ruin; it is, in fact, the only mission in California which, from its earliest days, has never been untenanted by Franciscans.

Some of the ruined missions suffered their first blows, not from secularization, but from the severe

seismic shocks of 1812 — *el año de los temblores.*
Chief of these was the vast cruciform building of
San Juan Capistrano, which succeeded the small
mission built by Serra. Before its ruins, in point of
beauty, even the unblemished pile of Santa Barbara must give way. The great cross, shattered
now, with its church, monastery, convent, and
workshops and its wings of corridors outlined, was
erected of gray stone and was hardly less than a
decade in building. On a mountain several leagues
away the great timbers for the beams were hewn.
The stone came from a quarry six miles distant.
The huge blocks were transported by the mission
Indians, numbering roughly a thousand, in crude
bullock-carts; the smaller blocks men, women, and
even children carried on their heads. Back and
forth in the daylight hours, year after year, the Indians of Capistrano trod the long way to bring the
stone that should build an imperishable shrine.
Imperishable, in one sense, it is; but its structure,
completed in 1806, stood unmarred for only six
years. One of the uninjured rooms of the convent
was converted into a chapel. Services are held
there and the parish priest lives at the mission.

About San Juan Capistrano, even today, lingers
the fragrance of the past. In the little seaside

village, Spanish, with Mexican accent, Basque, and
Portuguese are more commonly heard than English.
In fact, English is seldom heard. The sombrero
frequently, and even an occasional dingy and
frayed serape, may be seen in the groups of swarthy
skinned men lounging and smoking in the sun.
Not far from the railway — which connects San
Diego with Los Angeles by a swifter route than the
old trail of the padres — in the mouth of the valley,
the majestic ruin stands. Gone is the high bell-
tower, once visible, so it is said, from ten miles
away. The roofs have crumbled in places, and the
gray walls and the thick square columns of the
arches are fissured from the temblor which destroyed the lofty church and crushed out the lives
of several hundred worshipers. Grasses and
weeds push their way through the broken floorings
and riot with the blazing California poppy in the
patios. Busy little birds, swift of wing and incessant in song, pop in and out of a village of nests in
the deserted corridors. Lazy doves, bronze and
blue and snow-white, float up from the street along
the sparkling bay to sun and plume themselves on
the ruined arches. And the lizard, though unattended by the lion, keeps the court. But the
dark vulture, wheeling above San Juan, wings

slowly on; for the stillness here is too old to be of the dead. It is the placidity of beauty, which is immortal.

In their pagan days the Indians of Capistrano honored the moon. Padre Boscana has preserved in his writings the refrain of the song sung at the feast and dance with which they greeted her: "As the moon dies and comes to life again, so we, having to die, shall live again." Night is still the feast of beauty at Capistrano. It is a feast kept now in silence — with the stately dance of a tribe of shadows moving through the arches to the slow rhythm of the rising moon. So does a vanished people "live again" in the supreme loveliness of their wrecked handiwork.

Colonization in California proceeded steadily, if slowly. California was far away and equally good lands could be had in Mexico. Spaniards lacked some of the incentives which stirred Englishmen to emigrate to the shores of the Atlantic. They attained to little greater degree of personal freedom and little larger share in their own government in a frontier presidio than in the City of Mexico or in Seville. Distance, of course, often made them independent for a time. But the heel of absolutism was on their necks wherever they went, and those who came lacked incentives to energetic industry. The land was too fertile; too much was done for them. Colonists were paid a salary for a term of years, given lands, stock, tools, in fact every necessary but the normal stimulus to labor. In California, where the climate compelled no measures of protection and the soil produced abundantly without urging, the spirit of *dolce far niente* possessed the settlers. Even the later coming of well-to-do families, who boasted the purest blood of Spain, made little change in the life of happy, sunny ease. Sheep and cattle increased, roamed the green valleys and found their own sustenance, with little effort on the part of their owners. Olive trees, introduced by the padres, flourished; and grain yielded from fifty to a hundredfold from a single sowing. Why work? Why be "progressive"? The implements used in cultivation were of the most primitive design. As late as '49 the Californians were ploughing, and happily, with an iron point attached to a crooked branch. The labor of field and range was done by Indians for a share of the produce. The lord of the hacienda was chiefly engaged in riding, in gambling, dancing, in visiting or receiving his friends, or attending bull and cock fights. There was indeed little else for him to do. The Government did not solicit his coöperation. He might, and often did, stir up a little revolution. If he had a mind to trade, he must pay a tithe on all transactions; and there were no markets for his stock, so that frequently he must slaughter great numbers of sheep, cattle, and horses to reduce his herds. He was not always devout, but he obeyed perfunctorily the laws relative to religious observances and left the rest to the virtue and piety of his women. Intellectually, his life was perforce sterile; for California was isolated; books there were none, and education was not greatly encouraged. Reversing the proverbial admonition, he seldom did today what he could put off till tomorrow: *mañana* was time enough for a task; now was for pleasure. And no pleasure was keener than bestriding a fine horse. His days were lived in the saddle; and his feats of horsemanship provoked the envy and admiration of early American and European travelers who have recorded them. To the end of Mexican days the Californians sustained the reputation brought by Rivera's men at the birth of the province — "the best horsemen in the world."

Though changing fashions in the outside world

affected the dress of the upper class, the Californians, generally, clung to their own style of garb.
The *caballero* who rode forth to take part in one of
the numerous fiestas at Monterey or San José was
attired in a jacket trimmed with scarlet, a brightly
colored silk sash, velvet pantaloons slashed below
the knee and laced with gilt, embroidered shoes, a
sombrero sporting a band of embroidery or ribbon
under which his head was tightly bound with a
black silk handkerchief. A serape was draped
about his shoulders; his long hair was braided in a
queue and tied with ribbons. Ribbons and jingling
bits of metal on bridle-reins and stirrups added to
the pride of his high-mettled horse. The sloe-eyed
maid who challenged him to dance by breaking on
his head a *cascarón* — an eggshell filled with gold
and silver paper, or scented water — would be arrayed in white muslin smock and petticoat flounced
with scarlet — her arms bare and her trim ankles
visible — scarlet sash, shoes of velvet or of blue
satin; and a gay *rebozo* or cotton scarf, in the man-
agement of which she would display an infinite
number of enticing and graceful gestures. When
the day's sports were over, the thin sweet twanging
of guitars would call *caballero* and *señorita* to the
dance, until, by ones and twos and whispering,

laughing groups, the merrymakers flitted home
like shadows across the plaza which lay white as
pearl in the drenching light of the southern moon.

The houses of the well-to-do in country or in
town were built about a court. The rooms opened
on a corridor which ran round the court, where
usually brilliant flowers grew and a fountain sent
up its rainbow sparkle. The poorer ranch houses
were of the plainest design and ill-furnished. The
people lived out of doors and gave little thought to
the interior of their dwellings. They built their
large rambling one-story houses of adobe with red
tile roofs, sometimes coating the outside walls with
whitewash and the inner with plaster. The poorer
houses had no floors but the hard earth and no
furniture except a chair or two with rawhide seats,
a bed of the same material, and a wooden bench
which was fixed along the wall. The hacienda was
overrun with Indian servants, frequently hired
from the missions, who did whatever work the
benign sun and soil had left for human hands
to do.

But if the Californian was idle and, as the padres
sometimes complained, not over-virtuous, he was
kindly and hospitable to a fault. His house and
all he possessed were free to friend and stranger for

a day or a year. No guest could wear out a Californian's welcome. If the guest were a poor man, on the day of his departure he would find a little heap of silver coins in his room from which he was thus silently bidden to ease a need his host had too much delicacy to mention. Horses would be provided for his journey to the next hacienda, where he would meet with the same treatment.

It was the opinion of travelers of that time that the Californians were superior to other Spanish colonists in America, including the Mexicans. And the superiority was variously ascribed to the greater degree of independence, social at least if not political, which they had attained through their far removal from Mexico and their lack of intercourse with the other colonies; and to the fact that, after the first settlements were made, the great majority of new colonists were of good Castilian blood; and to the influence of California itself. However that may be, the life of the Californians presented phases not always seen in Spanish colonies. The beauties and graces of the Spanish character flowered there; and the harsher traits were modified. Perhaps the Californian bull fight may be cited as typical of this mellower spirit, for it lacked the sanguinary features which characterized the national sport in Mexico and Spain. The quarry retired from the arena not much the worse for a chase which had served chiefly to exhibit the dexterity and horsemanship of the *toreador*.

After the inrush of Americans, who, paradoxically enough, stumbled upon the gold which Spaniards had vainly sought, this leisurely life inevitably passed away. California of our time commemorates the day when a people possessed by the energy of labor came to the Golden Gate. But it still bears, indelibly stamped upon it, the imprint of Spain.

BIBLIOGRAPHICAL NOTE

No single work covers the entire field of this book. Numerous topics are well treated in Justin Winsor, *Narrative and Critical History of America*, volumes II and III (1889), whose bibliographies are even better than its essays. Broad in scope and scientific in spirit are John Gilmary Shea's *History of the Catholic Missions Among the Indian Tribes of the United States, 1529–1854* (1855), and *The Catholic Church in Colonial Days, 1521–1763* (1886). Original documents covering a wide range of subjects for the sixteenth and seventeenth centuries are contained in Pacheco and Cárdenas (*et al.*), *Colección de Documentos inéditos, Relativos al Descubrimiento, Conquista, y Colonización de las Posesiones Españoles*, 42 vols. (1864–1884), and *Colección de Documentos Inéditos de Ultramar*, segunda série, 13 vols. (1885–1900).

A number of works, though not general, deal with considerable portions of the field. For the Atlantic seaboard there is Peter J. Hamilton, *The Colonization of the South* (1904). In Spanish there is Don Gabriel de Cárdenas Z. Canos (anagram for Don Andrés Gonzalez Barcía), *Ensayo Cronologico para la Historia General de la Florida* (1723), which, though annalistic, is broader in scope than any subsequent treatment of Florida. It covers the Atlantic and Gulf areas from 1512 to 1722.

The Southwest is best covered by the various volumes of Hubert Howe Bancroft's *Works*. The parts relating to the Spaniards, which were written mainly by Henry Oak, are an unsurpassed mine of information. A popular introduction to Spanish activities in the Southwest, vigorous and entertaining in style, is Charles F. Lummis, *Spanish Pioneers* (1893). The same region is covered with emphasis on colonizing methods in Frank W. Blackmar, *Spanish Institutions of the Southwest* (1891). An excellent eighteenth century work in Spanish is Juan Domingo de Arricivita, *Chrónica Seráfica y Apóstolica del Colegio Propaganda Fide de la Santa Cruz de Querétaro* (1792). It was written by an official chronicler who had been a missionary in Texas. A general documentary collection is Herbert E. Bolton, *Spanish Exploration in the Southwest, 1542-1706* (1916).

EARLY EXPLORATION. Aside from these few general and regional works, most of the materials are special, and can be listed according to the chapters of this book. Early sixteenth century explorations are admirably treated in Woodbury Lowery, *Spanish Settlements Within the Present Limits of the United States, 1513–1561* (1901). Popular accounts of the exploration of Florida are Graham, *Hernando de Soto* (1903), Grace King, *De Soto and his Men in the Land of Florida* (1898), and, though old, Theodore Irving, *The Conquest of Florida by Hernando de Soto* (1835). The standard treatise on Coronado is George Parker Winship, *The Coronado Expedition, 1540–1542* (*Fourteenth Annual Report of the Bureau of Ethnology*, 1896). Contemporary narratives are contained in Hodge and Lewis,

Spanish Explorers in the Southern United States (Original Narratives of Early American History, 1907); Ad. F. and Fanny Bandelier, *The Journey of Cabeza de Vaca (Trail Makers Series*, 1905); Pedro Castañeda and others, *The Journey of Coronado (Trail Makers Series*, 1904), edited by George Parker Winship. Edward Gaylord Bourne, *Narrative of the Career of Hernando de Soto (Trail Makers Series*, 1904); Buckingham Smith, *Colección de Varios Documentos para la Historia de la Florida* (1857). Garcilaso de la Vega, *La Florida del Ynca* (1605).

EARLY FLORIDA. Menéndez de Avilés is the theme of Woodbury Lowery's second volume, *Spanish Settlements Within the Present Limits of the United States, 1562–1574* (1905). A graphic and scholarly account of the expulsion of the French by Menéndez is given by Francis Parkman in his *Pioneers of France in the New World* (1865). Documentary collections are E. Ruidíaz y Caravía, *La Florida, su Conquista y Colonización por Pedro Menéndez de Avilés* (1893), and Genaro García, *Dos Antiguas Relaciones de la Florida* (1902).

NEW MEXICO. Spanish New Mexico can be studied in Hubert Howe Bancroft, *Arizona and New Mexico* (1888), and Ralph Emerson Twitchell, *Leading Facts of New Mexican History*, vol. I (1911). Antiquated but useful is W. W. H. Davis, *Spanish Conquest in New Mexico* (1869). Mission antiquities are treated in L. Bradford Prince's beautifully illustrated *Spanish Mission Churches of New Mexico* (1915). The authority on the Pueblo Revolt is Charles W. Hackett, who has published several scholarly papers on the subject.

based on manuscript materials, in the *Southwestern Historical Quarterly* and *Old Santa Fé*. An excellent regional study is Anne E. Hughes, *Beginning of Spanish Settlement in the El Paso District* (1914). A contemporary account of Oñate's work by an eyewitness is Gaspár de Villagrá, *Historia de la Nueva Mexico* (1610), which is written in verse. A rare picture of New Mexico in 1630 is Alonso de Benavides, *Memorial*, translated by Mrs. Edward E. Ayer and annotated by Frederick Webb Hodge and Charles F. Lummis (1916). Documents are contained in Ralph Emerson Twitchell, *The Spanish Archives of New Mexico*, 2 vols. (1914), and Herbert E. Bolton, *Spanish Exploration in the Southwest, 1542–1706* (1916), where extensive recently discovered material is presented.

PIMERÍA ALTA AND BAJA CALIFORNIA. The work of the Jesuits in Pimería Alta and Baja California is treated in Hubert Howe Bancroft's *North Mexican States*, 2 vols. (1883–89), his *Arizona and New Mexico* (1888), Fr. Zephyrin Engelhardt, *The Missions and Missionaries of California*, vol. I (1908), and Theodore H. Hittell, *History of California*, vol. I (1885). An interesting popular book, of slight historical merit, however, is Arthur North, *The Mother of California* (1908). Excellent eighteenth century accounts are José Ortega, *Apostólicos Afanes de la Compañía de Jesús* (1754); Miguel Venegas, *Noticia de la California*, 3 vols. (1757); and Francisco Xavier Alegre, *Historia de la Compañía de Jesús*, 3 vols. (1841). The foundational source for Kino's work is his own *Historical Memoir of Pimería Alta* (1919) edited by Herbert E. Bolton.

TEXAS. The only general sketch of Spanish Texas is contained in Garrison's *Texas, A Contest of Civilizations* (1903). More detailed, for the ground covered, are R. C. Clark, *The Beginnings of Texas* (1907), William Edward Dunn, *Spanish and French Rivalry in the Gulf Region of the United States, 1678–1702* (1917); and Herbert E. Bolton, *Texas in the Middle Eighteenth Century* (1915). Of the four named only the last two are based on adequate materials. Documents and monographs by Austin, Bolton, Buckley, Clark, Cox, Dunn, Marshall, McCaleb, and others are in the *Texas State Historical Association Quarterly* and the *Southwestern Historical Quarterly*. The story of the French border is told by Francis Parkman in his *La Salle and the Discovery of the Great West* (1910), and his *Half Century of Conflict* (1892), and Pierre Heinrich, *La Louisiane sous la Campaignie des Indes* (1905). Contemporary narratives are Alonso de León, *Historia de Nuevo León* (edited by Genaro García, in *Documentos Inéditos*, xxv, 1909), and Fr. Isidro Felix de Espiñosa, *Chrónica Apostólica y Seráphica de Todos los Colegios de Propagande Fide* (1746). Espiñosa was long a missionary on the Río Grande and in Eastern Texas. Documents are contained in Bolton's *Spanish Exploration in the Southwest*, and in Estéban L. Portillo, *Apuntes para la Historia Antigua de Coahuila y Texas* (1886).

ALTA CALIFORNIA. Histories of Alta California are numerous. The best general repositories of facts are the works of Bancroft, Hittell, and Engelhardt. Elementary sketches are Rockwell D. Hunt, *California the Golden* (1911) and H. K. Norton, *The Story of*

California (1913).   The results of recent scholarship
are presented in Irving B. Richman, *California under
Spain and Mexico* (1911), for which the archive materials were gathered mainly by Bolton; Charles Edward
Chapman, *The Founding of Spanish California* (1916);
and Herbert Ingram Priestley, *José de Gálvez* (1916).
Zoeth Eldredge, *The Beginnings of San Francisco*
(1912), gives an excellent account of the Anza expeditions.   Francisco Palóu's *Noticias de la Nueva California*
(1874), and his *Junípero Serra* (1787, English translation, edited by G. W. James, 1913), are excellent contemporary accounts.   Documents are in Elliott Coues,
On the Trail of a Spanish Pioneer, 2 vols. (1900), and
in various volumes of the Academy of Pacific Coast
History *Publications*.

LOUISIANA.   The sketches of Louisiana under Spain
have been thus far mainly written with attention fixed
on New Orleans.   Useful accounts are in Albert Phelps,
Louisiana (1905), Charles Gayarré, *History of Louisi-
ana* (1903), vol. III, Reuben Gold Thwaites, *France in
America* (1905), pp. 281-295; F. A. Ogg, *The Opening
of the Mississippi* (1904), pp. 294-459; Barbé-Marbois,
History of Louisiana (English translation, 1830); W. R.
Shepherd, *The Cession of Louisiana to Spain* (*Political
Science Quarterly*, XIX), 439-458; Herbert E. Bolton,
*Athanase de Mézières and the Louisiana Texas Frontier,
1768-1780*, 2 vols. (1914), vol. I, Introduction.   Peter
J. Hamilton, *The Colonization of the South* (vol. III of
G. C. Lee's *History of North America*, 1904); *Colonial
Mobile* (1910) by the same author; Louis Houck, *His-
tory of Missouri*, 3 vols. (1908); Thomas M. Marshall,
History of the Western Boundary of the Louisiana

Purchase, 1803–1841 (1914). Documentary collections are Louis Houck, *The Spanish Régime in Missouri,* 2 vols. (1909); James Alexander Robertson, *Louisiana under the Rule of Spain, France, and the United States,* 2 vols. (1911); and Bolton's *Athanase de Mézières,* just cited.

THE ANGLO-SPANISH BORDER. The materials for the Anglo-Spanish border are still scattered and are to be found chiefly in the separate histories of the West Indies, South Carolina, Georgia, and Florida, and of the intercolonial wars. Especially useful are the works of Shea and Barcía, already cited, and Sir William Laird Clowes (and others) *The Royal Navy,* 7 vols. (1897–1903).

INDEX

305